FTL

TODD DALLAND NICHOLAS GOLDSMITH

National Symphony Orchestra Acoustical Shell, Washington DC, 1979

Architectural Monographs No 48

FTL TODD DALLAND NICHOLAS GOLDSMITH

SOFTNESS MOVEMENT AND LIGHT

ROBERT KRONENBURG

A.D. ACADEMY EDITIONS

For Frei Otto and Ted Happold: mentors, friends and partners.
Todd and Nicholas

Acknowledgements
I first visited FTL's office in Manhattan in 1993. At that time I was coming to terms with the way in which temporary places generate feelings in people that are no less powerful than permanent ones and what that means for the future of architectural design. I had seen the Carlos Moseley Music Pavilion and was fascinated by this dramatic structure, which was created without any of the typical 'building' conventions. FTL's office was filled with hundreds of models of buildings and structures that attempted to do this for all types of function, with widely differing budgets in diverse environments. This meeting with Nicholas Goldsmith, and my later discussions with him and Todd Dalland, convinced me that here were designers who recognised no limits to what lightweight, temporary or portable architecture could achieve. Working in their office during the preparation of this book, surrounded by thousands of images of buildings that used the most advanced materials to make beautiful organic shapes, with a view to the north of the Chrysler building, to the south of the World Trade Center, and to the west – easily missed between huge permanent structures – FTL's delicate tensile structure for the ferry terminal at the World Financial Center, was one of the best experiences I have ever had. I would like to thank Nick and Todd for their trust in placing in my hands something that is so important to them, Maggie Toy of Academy Editions for her advice and commitment to the project, and my wife Lisa for her invaluable support during its preparation.

The experience of writing and editing this monograph has led me to the conclusion that this is just the first book on FTL's work – they have a lot more to do, and what they do is of the future.

Robert Kronenburg, March 1997
University of Liverpool

All illustrative material for this book was supplied to the publisher by FTL. Among the photographs from this source are images by: Jeff Goldberg, Esto Photographics pp16, 62, 63, 66 (top); Institut Für Leichte Flächentragwerke (IL) p8; Loie Fuller p7 (right); Graphics by Keith Goddard/Studioworks p51; Elliott Kaufman pp6, 89, 90, 92, 93, 94, 96, 98, 100, 101, 102-103; Jennifer Krogh p51; Chris Lee p60; M Lent Photography pp12 (top right), 16 (top right), 17 (top left), 38, 40, 76 (top right), 82 (top and bottom right); Kelly Mooney p2; William Neil p13; Bo Parker p12; Durston Saylor pp15, 17, 22, 87; David Wood p46. All other photographs are © FTL/Happold.
Attempts have been made to locate the sources of all photographs to obtain full production rights, but in the very few cases where this process has failed to find the copyright holder, apologies are offered.

Cover: Michael Lent, Atlanta Olympic Games, 1996.

Architectural Monographs No 48

First published in Great Britain in 1997 by
ACADEMY EDITIONS
a division of John Wiley & Sons,
Baffins Lane, Chichester,
West Sussex PO19 1UD

Other Wiley Editorial Offices
New York • Weinheim • Brisbane • Singapore • Toronto

Distributed to the trade in the United States of America by
NATIONAL BOOK NETWORK, INC
4720 Boston Way, Lanham, Maryland 20706

ISBN 0-471-97693-8

Printed and bound in Singapore

CONTENTS

INTRODUCTION
Robert Kronenburg

Todd Dalland FAIA, right, and
Nicholas Goldsmith FAIA, left

*Outside the very real tasks, we were bound, in particular,
by the search for the unobtainable objective. We wanted
to discern the developing, unstatic, never-completed
nature in its entire reality and beauty …*

*Our route was a narrow, bumpy path in unknown territory
with an unknown objective in the search for a possible,
minimalist architecture, an architecture of the obvious and
technically correct, without a claim to the sole correctness
of the path.*
Frei Otto[1]

From where will a new architecture emerge? In the course
of the twentieth century there have been many hopeful
beginnings and few fulfilled promises. The idea that the
dramatic changes of this century could really have a
complementary architectural form, which somehow both
represents and communicates the deep sociological, cultural
and technological revolution that society has experienced.
It possesses a powerful and persistent fascination – a
fascination that drove Frei Otto and his collaborators, and
continues to inspire others today.[2] Architecture is the one
creative form that synthesises the diverse currents of human
thought and experience. If it is found to be powerless in
creating a meaningful new manifestation at this critical
point in human development, then surely it also means
that humankind is powerless to keep up with its own pro-
gression. For this reason the premise that there is a form
of architectural *Zeitgeist* which is a quintessential, root
component of human existence is too important to discard.

If it is accepted that this idea cannot be relinquished,
where can an appropriate starting point for the search be
found? The basic patterns of architectural form have been
laid down in recognisable systems that have remained
unchanged for millennia – people are basically the same
size and have the same senses and physical perceptual
abilities as when they first began to build many centuries
ago. This is a major reason why history has been a rich
resource for new architectural development. It is, however,
a characteristic of human nature to ignore the parts of history which do not accord with the current image it seeks.

The Renaissance saw ancient classical architecture
(through a fortunate availability of information on its form)
used as a resource for interpreting the recent changes in
society and the establishment of a new creative vigour.
Until relatively recently, twentieth-century architectural
commentators have ignored the importance and relevance
of traditional vernacular forms. They have overlooked their
response to the environments and circumstances in which
they were created and also disregarded them as precedents for the built forms which have subsequently shaped
the architectural mainstream.[3] In this century there has
been a plethora of stylistic forms, many of which have
sought inspiration from the past. However, in many cases
the selective parts of the past used have been raided for
images rather than the meaning the buildings possessed
in their context. Before looking once more to the past,
present-day architects therefore need to carefully examine
the current, and if at all possible, the future context in
which they build.

Perhaps the greatest influence on the contemporary
world is technological progress. At different times perceived as saviour and suppressor of the human race, it
nevertheless appears to be unstoppable. It can reasonably
be argued that the true story of present-day architecture
began with the Industrial Revolution, though many buildings since then still seem to have been created with an
image that completely ignores its impact. The most clearly
visible examples of its effect are those structures which
have been developed to serve industry. Engineering-led
building designs have been recognised before, for their
immediacy in response to new technologies, and hailed
for being advanced (though of course they were generally
still years behind the actual technological developments
which led to their existence). Reyner Banham argued that
the separation between architecture and technology had
a crippling effect on the development of this the most
all-enveloping of the arts. In particular it was the new
ingredients of building design, the environmental modi-
fiers, such as electricity, air conditioning and ventilation,
that architects lost control of, rather than the modern
replacements for outdated structural systems.[4]

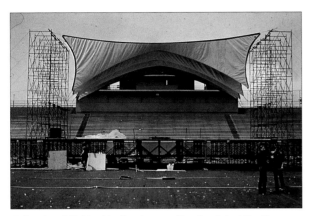

Dalland and Goldsmith cleaning up after the riot at the Deep Purple Concert, E–Z Builders, Cornell Football Stadium, 1973

Evocation of dynamic tensile form, Loie Fuller in the 1890s

Though there were precursors, most architects finally became fascinated with technology in the twentieth century; in many cases, however, even among famous and influential designers, the effect on the appearance of the building was of greater concern than the development of an architecture with forms more appropriate to human needs. [5] The recent manifestation of high-tech can confidently be described as stylistically led, as many buildings of this type indicate their designers' fascination with the imagery of technology rather than its essence. The appropriate use of technology is primarily about doing things that were not possible before, or doing what was previously possible more efficiently and more economically. The cynical observer might conclude that shiny, connectable, bolt-on bolt-off imagery is just that – imagery. In many instances real technology is invisible, or if not invisible getting smaller all the time. Large computers become small computers which become minute processors. The less physical material you use the less material costs go into the making of an object and less of the Earth's resources are used. Eventually (though usually not straight away) it becomes a long-term prospect for greater economy. This real technology of the 'almost not there' is the true innovation of the twentieth century, and as good a place as any to start looking for an inspiration for a new architecture. In this case, its precedents in the past are also quite clear.

The technology of tensile-membrane structures is perhaps the most potent example of contemporary building engineering that utilises new materials and new techniques. Though based on structural strategies that have been understood for millennia, it is only in the second half of the twentieth century that its potential has begun to be realised as a direct result of the development of new materials.

Todd Dalland, founding partner of FTL, became fascinated with tensile structures in the seventies while at architecture school at Cornell. At that time there was a feeling among the students in American universities that the world really could be changed – there was a new sense of getting in touch with what really mattered. One manifestation of this among architecture students was a new interest in alternative technologies and the work of Buckminster Fuller, who had long been an advocate of holistic thinking and the benefits of lightweight technologies. *Domebook*, which later was revised and updated as *Shelter*, was an immensely influential, alternative building handbook. It identified and made understandable a wide range of simple, yet effective, traditional building methods from around the world, set them in context and updated them by suggesting readily available local materials. [6] In 1971, while in his second year at Cornell, Dalland convinced a local realtor to sponsor him and fellow classmates Denis Hector and Alex Neratof to form a design studio called E–Z Builders, which would explore the potential of inflatable, space-frame and tensile-structure technology as a basis for inexpensive student housing. That summer, Dalland and Hector hitchhiked to New York City to see Frei Otto's full-scale tensile structure erected in the courtyard of the Museum of Modern Art. [7] A week later they had built their first tensile structure, and within a month completed larger tensile structures for their first client, the University Without Walls at Amherst, Massachusetts. Fellow classmate Nicholas Goldsmith joined soon after, and the group continued their independent practice designing and building tensile structures for their own clients throughout their architectural education. The main thrust of Cornell's architecture courses at this time had been defined by Colin Rowe and the young tutors he had brought from Texas A&M (nicknamed the Texas Rangers), who developed a very strong Modernist Corbusian theme throughout the student work. Though they were encouraged by the Visual Studies Professor, Gene Messick, and the Structures Professor, Donald Greenberg, Dalland, Goldsmith and Hector received their formal education during the day and continued to design and make tensile structures primarily in the evenings and at weekends. They used inexpensive materials available from the local hardware store such as polythene, fibre tape, polyester ropes and aluminium tube. Conrad Roland's book *Frei Otto: Tension Structures* served as a resource for exploring tensile-structure forms and technology. [8] The group were also influenced by engineer-builders such as Felix Candela,

Frei Otto, Jeddah Sports Centre at King Abulazziz University, 1978

Future Tents Limited, White House Ellipse Canopies, 1979

Frei Otto, Pink Floyd Umbrellas for the 1976 USA tour

E–Z Builders, Ring Tent on Arts Quadrangle, Cornell, 1972

Todd Dalland, Thesis model, Cornell, 1974

Future Tents Limited, Aspen Windstar, 1980

Future Tents Limited, Norwalk In-Water Boat Show, 1977

The first rental tensile structure, Anchor Modules 40' Wide, Future Tents Limited, 1978

Pier Luigi Nervi and Robert Maillart, as well as by experimental architects, such as Norman Foster, Paolo Soleri and the Archigram Group.

Between 1971 and 1975 the team completed several full-size projects, including a concert shell for the football stadium at Cornell and a memorial for a fellow student in Auburn, New York State.[9] In 1975 Dalland and Goldsmith took their final thesis projects advised by tutor Kent Hubbell (also a tensile-structure designer and now Chairman of the College of Architecture, Cornell). Dalland's study explored mathematical form-finding and cutting patterns for double-curved surfaces, which he investigated with the aid of a programmable desktop calculator and demonstrated with scale-fabric models. Goldsmith's thesis concerned a town-centre redevelopment for Anchorage, Alaska, in which he proposed large-scale fabric structures that would moderate the extreme environment and enhance outdoor public activity. Shortly after they left university, Denis Hector and Nicholas Goldsmith went to Germany to work directly with Frei Otto, and Dalland founded his own company making tents and lightweight structures. In 1977, Todd Dalland formed Future Tents Limited with his engineer brother Ross Dalland. They bought two large industrial sewing machines, which they used to make the tensile structures they designed and installed, and an IBM typewriter. That year they made two 300-square-metre tensile canopies for the national Norwalk In-Water Boat Show in Connecticut. Jerry O'Connell of the commercial tent-rental company HDO, who supplied most of the marquees for the show, saw the dramatically unconventional design created by the Dalland brothers and was impressed enough to introduce them to John Daus of Anchor Industries, a major manufacturer of standard marquee structures. Daus understood the potential of their innovative designs and commissioned Future Tents to develop a set of technically new, tensile-structure patterns, which could be introduced into the commercial tent-rental industry.

Nicholas Goldsmith stayed in Germany for more than two years working with Otto on a range of projects, including the Munich Zoo Aviary, the Jeddah Sports Centre, the Pink Floyd Retractable Umbrellas and the Saudi Parliament building. There he learnt Otto's physical modelling techniques for developing complex tension structures and met engineers Ian Liddell, Michael Dickson and Eddie Pugh, who worked with Ted Happold at Ove Arup in London. Denis Hector left Germany after a few months and went to work in England at the University of Bath and at Buro Happold, which had been formed when Ted Happold left Ove Arup to set up a new engineering firm.[10] In 1978 Goldsmith returned to New York and joined Future Tents Limited, and was followed in early 1979 by Hector. By this time Anchor had commissioned the first rental, tensile-structure design – a design, patented by Future Tents, which is still manufactured today. In 1979, Future Tents won a contract to provide five tensile-structure pavilions, situated in the White House grounds in Washington, DC. HDO's O'Connell saw the pavilions being erected and invited Todd Dalland to attend a meeting concerning the design of a new band shell for the National Symphony Orchestra on the Capitol's West Lawn. From this chance event, Future Tents obtained its first nationally recognised commission situated on one of the most important civic spaces in the USA.[11]

Fabric cutting patterns for these early projects were mostly created using Ross Dalland's enhanced geometrical calculations on a programmable calculator. The patterns for one project, however, the Aspen Windstar, was designed by Goldsmith using physical modelling techniques (originally developed by Frei Otto) that involved the manufacture, loading and measuring of accurate small-scale prototypes. In 1980, these laborious methods were replaced as consulting services with Buro Happold led to the first version of their powerful computer software becoming available. As the firm's work diversified they abbreviated their name to FTL to avoid the impression that their design output was restricted solely to tents.[12] FTL continued to develop their integrated design approach involving both in-house engineers and a close link with the Buro Happold engineers, who were both friends and imaginative collaborators. In 1985, Denis Hector left the partnership to pursue a career in academic research and Ross Dalland left to set up his own engineering practice.

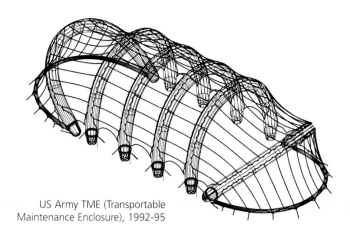

US Army TME (Transportable Maintenance Enclosure), 1992-95

US Army LANMAS (Large Area Night Maintenance Shelter), 1993

Todd Dalland and Nicholas Goldsmith remain principal partners of FTL, though the practice is now integrated with British engineers Buro Happold as FTL Happold Architects and Engineers, formalising a link previously established on a project by project basis. FTL Happold now design and engineer large-scale projects that involve permanent as well as relocatable structures. However, the partners' original creative philosophy also remains the same: to incorporate new materials and technologies into building design in a humanistic way; and to increase flexibility and responsiveness to programmatic requirements by encouraging the development of buildings and building components that move, and by striving for lightness by the use of minimal structures and open translucent spatial envelopes.

The practice has developed a design procedure for tensile structures that is based on an integrated method of physical model-making, computer modelling and practical experience. Initial sketches are created from ideas developing out of the programme. Almost immediately, three-dimensional physical work is begun, working to scale using mesh and fabric models. Often these are developed through many iterations that improve and detail the form. Once a satisfactory approach is reached the models are carefully measured and their dimensions – lengths of compression and tension members, radii of cables and fabric forms, angles and relationships between the different elements in the design – are transferred to the computer. Wind, snow and other imposed loads associated with construction and maintenance are then imposed on the computer model, which alters the design by the removal of excessive stresses. Changes are applied to the physical model, which may then generate further changes, that are then reapplied to the computer model. This process may be repeated many times during the design development as aesthetic and functional issues are brought to bear on the project. The last task that is undertaken on the computer is to develop a two-dimensional pattern that can be given directly to the membrane manufacturer, often on disk. FTL Happold use *Tensyl Suite*, an in-house software developed by Buro Happold, which provides form

generation, analysis, patterning and graphics.[13] The latest versions of the software operate up to sixty times faster than in the past, and much faster than in the early days when programmable calculators were used.

A particular concern of FTL is to develop and refine the details of tensile structures. Early tensile structures though beautiful in form were often crude in detail, a result of using technology that was still under development, but also of a lack of awareness of the importance of details as expressive elements in the new architecture that was being generated. Dalland believes that buildings, which are appreciated primarily through their visual presence, exhibit a form of body language akin to that experienced between human beings. The language of more traditional forms of architecture is well known to users either through familiarity with the past or common contemporary usage. New forms of architecture need to establish a new language which expresses its use and function as articulately as the old. To some extent, tensile structures already have a partial vocabulary – the traditional tents of North Africa have a romantic, nomadic image, which is familiar throughout the world, though there are undoubtedly inaccuracies in that image as it is largely acquired second hand. A more directly related perception of the tensile structure for most people is that of the circus tent, which is familiar to almost everyone, and is primarily a symbol of entertainment and event. These images are potent, and no doubt explain why the new tensile structures have been more readily accepted in some areas than others (particularly as event and performance structures). However, there is no pre-existing detail language. Where is the archetypal entrance to a circus tent? What is the tensile equivalent of a column base, a capital, an eaves line or a window sill? Dalland believes that this is one of the most important tasks for architects involved in the development of new tensile structures: the creation of a recognisable architectural language that will transform engineering into building, and building into architecture. In order to achieve this, the details that control and articulate the tensile and compressive forces, as well as the fabrics and membranes themselves, must become expressive of

Anchor Century 40' Tent, 1989

Armbuster 72' Tension Tent, 1991

Anchor Modules 60' Tents, 1982

Johnson Genesis 80' Tent, 1986

Omni/Guggenheim Museum Mobiles, New York, 1988

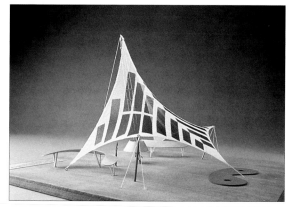

'Under the Sun' exhibition of photo-voltaic technology,
Cooper Hewitt National Design Museum, scheduled 1998

their function, of the materials in which they are made, and of the environment in which they exist. Ultimately, these components will become as refined as the fabric forms for which they provide the essential constructional connections.

If a new architectural form for the next millennium is to be found then it must be one that integrates change. For there is one thing that is certain about the events of the twentieth century, which will carry over into the next, and that is the dramatic escalation in both technological advances and their consequent effects on the way human-kind lives and inhabits the Earth. New and developing technologies are directly linked with tensile structures. The biggest innovation in tensile buildings has occurred in that invisible manner, in other words, through new materials that improve the capabilities of existing constructional strategies and also encourage and enable the development of new ones. Current three- and four-layer membranes will give way to lighter and stronger multi-layer materials. As well as the passive environmental modification utilised by membrane structures, new materials will also incorporate reactive and proactive systems that will include variable insulation, levels of translucency, communications and power generation. New construction and manufacturing techniques will also lead to greater efficiency in assembly and deployment.

FTL are involved in a number of projects that explore innovations such as this. The Transportable Maintenance Enclosure (TME) and Light Area Night Maintenance Shelter (LANMAS) projects are part of an ongoing research pro-gramme for the US Army carried out in collaboration with their Natick Research and Development establishment. These projects are speedily deployable mobile shelters that can be assembled and erected in minutes. They may be used for helicopter maintenance, barracks and a wide range of other military and civil functions. They utilise tensile membranes in conjunction with air-beam construction. Though this is not a new idea in itself, new high-strength, lightweight fabrics mean that the structures are extremely light and compact enabling easy transportation and, for the first time, once in use the structures will no longer

require constant air input to remain erect. The new materials enable smaller section beams to be used at higher air pressures, which means that deployment time can be measured in minutes rather than hours or days. A tensile structure that FTL are developing for the 'Under the Sun' exhibition at the Cooper Hewitt Museum of Design in New York (1998) also uses new technology to develop the capabilities of this building form. This portable exhibi-tion will use flexible photo-voltaic cells integrated into the tensile membrane, which will provide the power to operate the electronic and audiovisual components of the exhibition. Individual projects like this give some indication of the future for tensile architecture.

A core component in the future success of this type of architecture is the way in which design concepts are generated. All the design work that Dalland and Goldsmith do is fully integrated with the engineering; always struc-tural, it is also concerned with lighting, acoustics and the mechanical when required. This integration comes into play right from the outset of the design of each project, when the primary inputs into the form of the building are being evaluated and coordinated. Tensile architecture cannot be designed in any other way because it relies on materials and techniques which integrate structure and form.

FTL have naturally gained a reputation for their tensile-structure design work, which means that their experience in this area is most developed. However, the temporary and portable nature of much of their work has also led to them being approached as consultants on architectural work of an ephemeral or lightweight nature – though not necessarily utilising fabric structures. In projects that use conventional materials and construction methods they apply the same design techniques. In particular, three-dimensional modelling is used to explore both structure and form, and maintain an awareness of the nature of the materials with which they are dealing, and the possibility of incorporating new techniques from their specialist area.

Tensile architecture, even if it could be the basis for a new architectural form, will not be exclusive of other building techniques: the mainstream processes are the major part of the expanding continuum of architectural

Creeping Devil Cactus forming regular arrays of starbust patterns

development.[14] An important part of the development of tensile and membrane architectural forms is therefore the relationship that they have with other building mediums: what they can contribute to existing building forms, as well as what they can generate on their own as a new, independent architectural image. The relationship of soft organic shapes to hard-edged orthogonal ones is not an easy one to develop satisfactorily; however, there is ample precedent in the way that countless beautifully made rectangular buildings have complemented the undulating natural landscape. Tension structures possess a quality that can be recognised in nature. This is true of both their visual form (the natural patterns of the land and of the sky is mirrored in tensile buildings) and of the way that they have been generated (their efficiency is dependent on the natural shape of membranes deformed by forces in the most efficient way). Frei Otto in developing this strategy utilised natural structures such as soap bubbles, sand patterns, air-supported membranes and gravity-deformed chain-nets to discover the most efficient shapes available in nature. Tensile structures can be perceived as a man-made reproduction of naturally occurring form; and conventional compressive and bending structures as a foil to nature creating regular shapes rarely seen in the natural world. The idea of a man-made object in the landscape that creates a contrast with the natural and a focus for man's relationship with nature is one that has been used many times before; it is possible that this same concept can be applied to the relationship between this new architecture and the old. The concept of a harmonious relationship between the two therefore does not seem impossible. In this way, it may even be possible for the recognisable body language of traditional architectural forms to help generate the new body language of the innovative.

Complex spider's web of the Genus Cyrtophora

Free-form structures of nature are mimicked in the Rotork Pavilion, Poole, UK, 1980

Opposing spirals shape the sunflower florets

CONVERSATIONS WITH FTL
Peter McCleary

Future Tents Limited (FTL) began with the conjecture that in many disciplines concepts of materials, construction, space and time had changed, and they wished to participate in the uncovering of these new concepts in the field of architecture. Todd Dalland and Nicholas Goldsmith's questioning was drawn to the new technology of fabric roofs where material, structure and space were united as one. However, this tensile architecture seemed powerless against the tradition of millennia for masonry in compression and our century's predilection for steel and reinforced concrete in flexure.

Ventriloquists of a terrestrial architecture argue that it is the realm of earth moving and building mounds – tombs and temples – where the horizontal plane of the earth is given spatiality by excavation and vertical piling of stone on stone. It is an architecture of compression where matter is depicted through its mass, density, rigidity, permanence, durability, hardness, opacity and weight. The nineteenth and twentieth centuries, in response to the logic of steel, developed an arboreal architecture of flexural skeletal frames. Some twentieth-century architectural futurists borrowed concepts from the aquatic realm of sailing, the aerial realm of flight, and the principles of moving equipment. Others took guidance from the mechanics and development of natural forms.

Ships, planes, machines, anatomy, soap film and bubbles, beehives and spider webs seemed less determined to gravitate to the ground than to levitate into the air. This new architecture would be one of lightness, even weightlessness, mobility and ascension, where one might express the bodiless, no-thing-ness and invisible. Here the mass of material of the terrestrial would be replaced by the flow of forces of the seemingly immaterial, where the heaving of weight transforms into hovering in an undecided state of suspense between the earth and the sky. To make visible the invisible force field is an aspiration where one must leave behind the body, going beyond its thresholds to a condition where one validates the structure, not by the aesthetics of beauty, but by the sublime.

From the outset FTL accepted as a project for life the search for lightweight, or the lightest possible, structures that can provide human shelter. Their point of departure was Frei Otto's study of lightweight structures, in general, and tents, in particular.

The tent is a portable shelter composed of a fabric envelope stretched by a support structure of tension cords and compression poles. The simplest covertures are the canopy, umbrella, parasol, awning, papilio, pavilion, baldachin, tepee, Mongolian yurt, Bedouin black tent and the circus tent. Their role is to shield the occupant from the sun and gnats, and to define a transportable place. Shelters, to be portable, must be lightweight and foldable. To be lightweight infers that the applied wind and snow loads are of greater magnitude than the self-weight. Masonry structures are exactly the opposite. While gravity directs snow loads downwards, the force of wind flows in many directions and is not static; thus the appropriate structural configuration cannot be derived from experience of gravity structures. Just as gravity loads can be used to prestress and hence redirect undesired stresses, wind forces are used to advantage in sails, windmills and wings. Perhaps in the future, wind need not be a burden but will similarly be positively channelled to support tents.

The lightest, lightweight configuration is that of structures with a minimum volume. In the case of fabric structures, they have a minimum surface area and a material of maximum allowable stress. The highest stresses are achieved in tensile materials in the form of linear cable, rod or planar fabric. Since architects rarely invent or manufacture structural cables or textiles, FTL must wait patiently for the new strong materials; just as architects waited for mass-produced steel in the nineteenth century.

While optimum structural configurations, however, are in their infancy, the discovery of new configurations remains a possibility for the design professions. FTL was introduced to Frei Otto's empirical studies of such structures, and Buro Happold provided the engineering analysis for Otto and later for FTL. In their mutual search for minimal surface structures and materials of maximum tensile capacity, the late Ted Happold mentored the young FTL; and his partners, Ian Liddell and Eddie Pugh, collaborated

Anchor Modules, 1979, cutting pattern model

Structure as building, World Financial Center Ferry Terminal, New York, 1990

with Dalland and Goldsmith on many projects, finally forming the US practice of FTL Happold.

For several years I have collaborated with FTL Happold in two settings. At the University of Pennsylvania, we teach an architectural design studio on the theme of the emerging technology of tensile structures. Dalland, Goldsmith, Happold, Hector, Liddell and Pugh have all participated in these studies of the continuum, from materials through structural and constructional systems to space. In Dalland-Goldsmith's practice our discussions focus on the development of an architectural language for fabric structures. Our structured inquiry generates, for each project, an essential taxonomy and vocabulary of the parts and their relationships – proportional and compositional. Further, we attempt to explain and evaluate the essence of the architecture of textiles, and speculate on possible and probable futures for the architecture and engineering of fabric structures. Paradoxically, we feign practice in the University and construct theories in their practice.

First among those things we concluded from these collaborations is the study of the nature of materials. Many vernacular and small tents were surfaces constructed of animal skins or hides. For others, surface skins were woven by interlacing yarns spun from threads of animal hair, for instance, wool and vegetable fibres were fabricated into cloth, such as linen, jute and hemp. Many metals have been woven into a mesh or network fabric. More recent structural fabrics are woven with a substrate or underlying structural layer of synthetic fibres or filaments – polyester and fibreglass – and covered with a durable coating made out of PVC, PTFE, Teflon or silicone as protection from heat, light, fire and dirt.

Most fabrics are woven in two perpendicular directions, that is, the warp and the weft. The directionality of the fabric derives from the anthropomorphic movements of the loom, in other words, forward–reverse, up–down and left–right. The ratio of the fabric's warp to weft, its physical properties, is a measure of the isotropy of the weave. Fabric should be stressed biaxially in proportion to that isotropy. If the fabric is isotropic, that is to say, the warp and weft are equal in capacity, then soap film can

serve as an analogy to generate a minimum surface-area structural configuration. This set of anticlastic curved surfaces, which ensure equal biaxial stresses, give the well-known geometric modules of fabric systems. Among them are: the surface of catenaries or catenoid; the helicoid; and the saddle shapes of hyperboloids and the hyperbolic paraboloid. While the asymptotic lines of these minimal surface structures form orthogonal nets – as does the fabric – it is difficult to orient this hyperbolic geometry with the cuboidal space of the three-directional, orthogonal axes of most human activities. The introduction of the other set of orthogonal nets, namely, the system of involute and evolute curves, to the weaving of fabric and structure, will disorient even the most deconstructed mind and body.

If the fabric is anisotropic, in other words, the warp and weft are unequal in capacity, the isotropy of the structural and spatial geometry must be deformed proportionately. Thus the orientations of the geometric space results from the isotropy of the fabric (and vice versa), mediated by the form of the structural configuration. Some recent fabrics escape the two directional, anthropomorphic constraint of the loom and are woven in three directions. When triaxially stressed, the new set of web patterns (tessellations of triangles and hexagons at 120 degrees) reveals a new set of boundary conditions and generates a triaxial space. The 'monkey saddle' or isolated parabolic umbilic is one result of weaving triaxially. It has three ridges and three valleys and a mesh at 120 degrees. In most biaxial fabric structures it is possible to understand that the snow is supported by the sagging tension curvature of the ridge cables and the wind's uplift is held down by the valley cables. However in the 'monkey saddle' every normal section of the tension surface has a point of inflection, which almost prohibits any visual understanding of the flow of forces. Its visible structure is almost as complex as the invisible energies.

As fabric escapes the limits set by the isotropy of the loom and enters the field of prestressing forces, which are of greater magnitudes than wind and snow loads, fabric structures approach the essence of soap film (or soap

Partial deployment of fabric skin, Carlos Moseley Music Pavilion, New York, 1991

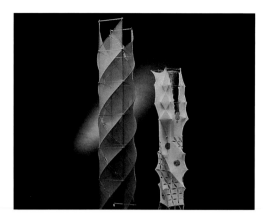

Fabric curtain-wall skyscrapers

bubbles, if the compression is supported by restrained air). FTL's statements that 'the structure is the building' and the 'force is the space' infer that the directionality of the material gives directionality to the structural configuration, which in turn gives the orientations, axes or directionality to space. Of course, once we have learned to build a large soap film, we must learn how to live in its space.

Just as we questioned the nature of materials, we also asked 'what does fabric want to be?'

The production of a space enveloped by fabric is a process of twisting and stretching – the structure of the fabric is determined by the interlacing. The raw material is spun, or twisted, or drawn out in one direction into a short fibre or long filament, then torqued in the opposite direction into yarn. A further reverse twists it into a strand and a final twist is needed for it to become a cord or rope, which intuitively is a linear fabric. Alternatively, the yarn can be knitted with no warp into a tension net; plaited or twined into a basket with a stiff compression warp and flexible tension weft; or woven into fabric or textile, which intuitively is a planar rope.

Textiles, nets and ropes are fabricated with soft, flexible yarns. Hence they are appropriate for clothes which envelope bodies that flex and move, and for portable tents that must be foldable. FTL is well aware of the pliability of fabrics and its relationship to movement. Goldsmith, recognising this deployability, calls their Carlos Moseley Music Pavilion (1991), 'the peripatetic pavilion'; the same is also true of The Time for Peace Pavilion (1994). These, and other projects, continue the tradition of mobile, flexible and temporary pavilions. Tents, where both the geometry of pliability and the system of flexors, which do the folding, need more careful study. The archi-tecture of textiles, not stone, is lithesome, not lithic – it is an architecture of mobility, made possible through folding.

Histories of the technologies of anthropology, archaeology and architecture have overemphasised lithic and metal tools, weapons and buildings at the expense of textile history. This androcentric bias, which favours male-centred over female-related technologies, perhaps accounts for the shortage of scholarly analysis of the textile

culture in architecture, Gottfried Semper's 1860 article on 'Style: The Textile Art' notwithstanding. Lack of durability is another factor.

Dalland asks: 'Is it a dress or a building?' Those industries that fashion clothes find similarities between FTL's intuition of material, surface and space and their own. Thus, Henri Bendel, Biederman, Liz Claiborne, Donna Karan, Calvin Klein, Issey Miyake and Carmelo Pomodoro sought FTL's expertise for the design of their showrooms and offices. Together, FTL and the Seventh Avenue Fashion Industry shared a panoply of fabric structures in their tented theatres for the Seventh on 6th Fashion Village at Bryant Park (1993-).

Not surprisingly, textile technology is one root of the language of fabric structures, and it is a source of ideas for the future. Perhaps the greatest insight into the correlation between new textiles and foldable structures has been displayed in the collections of Issey Miyake.

Civilian clothes tend to be soft, flexible, *prêt-à-porter*, degradable and lightweight, whereas protective military clothes, or armour, are hard, rigid, difficult to carry, durable and heavy. Once, tents were similar to civilian clothes, but today, in competition with permanent and durable buildings, they seek to armour themselves. Paradoxically, like chain mail, they wish to remain lightweight.

As materials, in general, and fabrics, in particular, derive their nature from the process of their production (that is, their directionality, or isotropy, results from weaving) so does structure derive its nature from its orientation in space. The layering of coatings, one for each environmental hazard, is the most basic armouring technique. Multiple laminations are the second-generation solutions. Is there a parallel to the historical development of 'curtain walls'? Fabric structures conceptualised as 'curtain roofs'. Both 'curtain' walls and roofs can be fabricated with either flexible or rigid materials. Dalland has proposed soft fabric curtain walls for skyscrapers. In the more distant future, both roof and wall will be self-regulating; made with cyber-fabrics or cyber-textiles.

The addition of mass through the use of coatings and laminations is the primal method of increasing local

Eureka! Genesis tent corner plates suggest the visualization of stresses

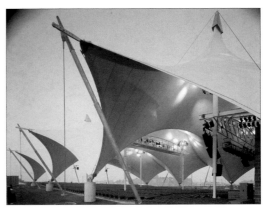

The push and pull of structure and space, Pier Six Concert Pavilion, Baltimore, MD, 1991

rigidity. Weaving or interlacing strips of the laminations will increase stiffness by increasing inertia without a proportionate increase in mass. This would be akin to weaving corrugated sheets. The top, outside surface, or extrados, would have a profile and physical properties different from the bottom, inside surface, or intrados. The first generation might be air-inflated.

The most common method to achieve rigidity against deformations caused by wind and snow is to twist or corrugate the fabric surface into an anticlastic curvature. This is done by warping the boundary stretcher frame, which remains outside the plane of the fabric surface. Another method uses compression members within that plane, for example, flying struts. This method is a precursor to a future system where a set of stiff compression members will interlace with soft, flexible, tensile, fabric strips. It is similar to Robert Le Ricolais' transformation of a flexible rope (or linear textile) into a stiff, hollow rope, where the tensile warp cables are wrapped around compressive weft diaphragms. It is a system more related to basketry than weaving.

The original tent was a portable shelter of fabric, stretched tight or tensed by a system of structural stretchers. Whereas we use the language of textiles to discuss the fabric, the stretcher frames of tension and compression members use the nautical language of rigging and loading sailing ships. The masts, jibs, booms, stays, tackle, winches, pulleys and so forth, together with the concomitant connections, are to be seen everywhere in fabric roofs.

The fabric, separated from the ground by the stretchers, expresses a surface of pure tension, beautiful and sublime as it hangs in the air, like a full sail, in an undecided state between the aerial and the arboreal, between the sky and the stretcher 'tree'. For the supported fabric to acquire the hovering state of suspense it requires a poised balance or equilibrium between tension and compression. Too much compression has the appearance of being 'grounded', and too much tension denies the concept of efficiency. FTL seeks to build finely tuned compositions.

Not unexpectedly, we noted that the directionality, orientations or isotropy of space correlate or mesh with those of structure. As in all structures, it is with the epistemology of the senses that we appropriate the logos of the building. The eye acts as a body at a distance measuring the push and the pull of the convex and concave, vertical and horizontal, sagging and hogging, straight and curved, parabola and catenary; all revealed or concealed in dark or light. Compression members threaten to fail in the free space around them, and inclined masts indicate exactly the path of their failure. Tension members promise to straighten, thus sagging ridge cables seem more secure than hogging valley cables. If the structure must deform, it should move around our space. FTL understands the push and pull of structure and space. The eye acts as a hand in imagining the manufacture of the weave of the fabric, the fabrication of the fabric roof and the spinning of the cables, and the stages in the assembly of the building. With imagination, one can hear the sounds of all the processes of production. The finely tuned ear can hear the stresses, their balance and the volumetrics of the space.

FTL know something fundamental about the poetics of building, that is that materials are woven, structural systems are woven, space is woven and the process of building is weaving.

Softness
ARCHITECTURAL BODY LANGUAGE
TENSILE WORK
Robert Kronenburg

These innovative structures demonstrated the possibility of reuniting the divergent fields of technology, art and philosophy – of mending the rift between architecture and engineering which is so prevalent in modern times.
Bodo Rasch[1]

Some architects and critics have difficulty in classifying tensile structures. This is largely because, in general, architectural training does not prepare designers for the challenge of manipulating non-rectangular forms.[2] The ultimate freedom from the restrictions of dealing with orthogonal forms can render the design process uncertain and threatening for those who have not been able to experience its special opportunities first hand. The feeling of being within a tensile structure is one that affects the senses deeply – a unique sensuous impression of gentle encapsulating light and natural enclosing space. This construction strategy enables the creation of unique and dramatic environments that cannot be created in any other way. A special feature of tensile membranes is that their form is completely integrated with their structure: the shape of the building is determined by the physical characteristics that maintain its strength, and that strength is achieved almost exclusively with tension forces. They are therefore almost unique in the range of construction materials, which usually rely on compression or bending forces. Fabric structures are simultaneously: supporting structure and building envelope, lighting system and acoustic environment, and environmental sculpture and architectural space. They form a building space which truly integrates interior and exterior with a minimum division between inside and outside. For this reason, they provide a unique opportunity for the exploration of truly integrated work that considers all the problems and opportunities of building design in one coordinated comprehensive procedure. The ultimate goal is for the design of a building that synthesises all the elements of construction and environmental control into a single fluid entity that not only performs satisfactorily but is also expressive of its design ambitions.

The structural system for tensile-membrane structures is based on the ability to accommodate prestressed loads either through air-support (usually uniformly spread, though with incipient air-beam technology this may change) or stiff-compression members (as point loads) sometimes combined with cables. The structure supports its own self-weight, but unlike most buildings this is a relatively small part of its total load which is primarily made up of imposed loads. Tensile strength in membranes is provided by a matrix of fibres. The simplest, traditional tensile buildings are made of animal skins or cloth fabricated out of animal hair. More efficient materials manufactured from plant fibre such as cotton or hemp woven into duck or canvas fabrics have been available for thousands of years.[3] In the twentieth century, synthetic fibres such as nylon, polyester, fibreglass and, most recently, carbon fibre have been utilised. Each of these new fabrics have their own specific characteristics which make them more suitable for some applications and less suitable for others. The main requirements of tensile fabrics are strength, non-combustibility and long life. Subsidiary requirements are low heat absorption, the availability of different translucencies (from high light permeability to completely opaque), resistance to dirt and easy cleaning, and ease of handling. The characteristics of different coatings such as Teflon and silicone play a large part in determining these qualities.

Fabrics have been used in building construction for centuries and yet because of a general disregard for the achievement of vernacular building systems the successful qualities of such buildings have largely been ignored. Fabrics can be used to make building envelopes that are much lighter than those formed by conventional means, and they have therefore primarily been used in situations where portability or speed of erection has been a requirement – mobile dwellings, military shelters and circus and other entertainment venues being most common. Contemporary fabric structures differ from all traditional types in one important way, in that the material is stretched until taut to impart additional strength to the structure. New materials and greater tolerances in construction have meant that modern tensile structures have a much greater capability than those in history.

Another precedent for tensile-membrane architecture is the dynamic hard structures that are expressive of natural forms. Art Nouveau designers such as Hector Guimard introduced sinuous organic shapes into architecture; however, when built in conventional materials, such as stone and timber, the physical object appeared in conflict with the expression the designer was trying to achieve. In contrast, Guimard's use of cast iron and glass enabled the creation of translucent structures such as the Metro-entrance canopies (built in Paris 1899-1904), which sometimes even utilised double-curved surfaces. In the 1920s, European Expressionists such as Hugo Häring began to explore the organic possibilities of architectural form and professed the desire, 'to examine things and allow them to discover their own images ... If we try to discover the "true" organic form, rather than to impose an extraneous form, we act in accord with nature.'[4] Häring's buildings made from heavyweight materials did not, however, express the relationship with natural forms that one might assume would derive from this approach. Hans Scharoun might be seen as the inheritor of Häring's vision, and though he used more plastic materials such as concrete to represent naturally formed spaces, the observer is left in no doubt as to the extent of the heavyweight man-made structures supporting his seductive surfaces. It is perhaps in the dynamic structures of Antoni Gaudí that organic shapes were most convincingly expressed. Though based on the compressive structural qualities of stone, many of his building forms were developed from hanging models that used weights suspended from cables and nets to create a structural 'negative' of the completed building.

The closest precedent for the spatial qualities of tensile-membrane architecture is that of the lightweight iron and glass structures, which first emerged in the nineteenth century – greenhouses, railway sheds, exhibition halls and galleria – where the concept of a continuous translucent skin first appeared. Such large, dramatic engineered structures provided the first concept of large-span, thin-skin enclosures that enabled a direct relationship to exist between structure and form, which was visible from both outside and inside the building.

The work of pioneers such as Frei Otto in Germany and Walter Bird in the US has profoundly influenced Nicholas Goldsmith and Todd Dalland. They readily acknowledge the seminal work which was done by such innovators on form generation in the early days, and also the remarkable buildings that were built using comparatively primitive materials and design techniques. However, they see the work of FTL as an attempt to take tensile-membrane building design to another level of expression. Designers of today inherit a relatively mature engineering form but an immature architectural expression. Dalland and Goldsmith perceive that their role is now one of developing a legitimate, understandable architectural expression for

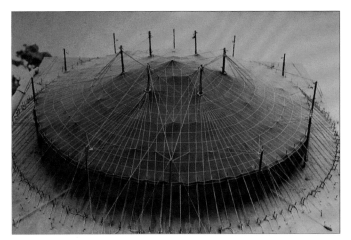
Hanging chain model of Antoni Gaudí's Colonia Güell Chapel (reconstruction by IL, Stuttgart, Germany)

Darien Lake Amphitheater, Buffalo, New York State, 1996

Bradford Exchange Offices and Exhibition, Chicago, 1985

Ringling Brothers' Traveling Arena, 1995

tensile buildings, which will enable them to become much more widely accepted and fulfil the potential that they believe this construction strategy possesses.[5]

During the twenty years that FTL have been in practice, the positive qualities of tensile architecture have come to be far more widely appreciated. This has been achieved in two major ways: by working directly with commercial manufacturers to develop and improve their product, and by targeting particular areas of architectural design that would benefit from the implementation of tensile-membrane buildings. Dalland's relationship with the commercial tent-making industry was established at the outset of his career and since that time he has worked directly with US manufacturers Anchor Industries, Eureka! and Armbruster. He has created a wide range of tent systems which have been sold to pragmatic business men, not on their visual appeal, though this has helped in some cases, but on purely practical grounds – swift erection, easy manufacture, modular assembly, a more usable and economic product. These tensile, commercial tenting systems now amount to 20 per cent of the total US market and are beginning to be used for more permanent, high-profile projects. Dalland's familiarity with these products has enabled him to use them in dramatic situations adapting standard products to large-scale events, such as the Bryant Park fashion shows in New York City and the US Olympic Games temporary infrastructure provision. Dalland has also been involved in writing the standard building codes for the industry.[6]

FTL's work for event structures originally began with commissions for low-cost temporary venues, often for sites that could not be released for long-term development. In these early projects the visual qualities of tensile structures were not fully realised by the clients until the project was completed. Now the opportunity of building a dramatic structure that will contribute to the quality and interest of the event it contains has often become part of the client's brief. However, the benefit of having flexible venues, which can be used for a wide range of events and can be erected with an extremely short lead-in time, is important to promoters who do not want to be restricted to conventional venues. These venues are sometimes designed to be dismantled once the summer season is over so that extreme, winter-weather conditions are avoided and they can therefore be made more economically. Event structures, such as this, have strong links with the circus tradition though they accommodate a far wider range of events and are more sophisticated in their use of interlocking technologies to present complex dramatic shows. They are also generally much larger structures, commonly seating four to five thousand people and visited by hundreds of thousands of people in each summer season. A current FTL project is for a Ringling Brothers' three-ring circus which will contain an 8,000-seat auditorium.[7]

In the search for a true architectural expression for tensile-membrane buildings FTL has developed a structural rationale based on more efficient layouts, which have in turn generated more refined building forms. Early tension structures tended to be free-form layouts that used compression members of varying height and skin shapes – their primary expression was of organic growth rather than efficient design. Though these buildings effectively conveyed the freedom of design possible with tensile membranes, their ad-hoc shape did not lead to a readily perceptible understanding of their form, either by the user or, even, other designers not privy to the form-generation criteria. FTL's recent work is directed towards balanced and harmonious shapes, often symmetrical in layout. There are practical benefits in this strategy, both in reducing the forces that determine the structure and in the manufacture of repetitive elements. It has, however, also resulted in shapes, which though still dramatic, have a clear order to them and can be distinguished from both inside and outside the building. Clearly defined, membrane shapes can also be used for more practical reasons – to create better acoustics in band-shell and auditorium design, and to focus attention on the stage area. The canopy for the music venue at Darien Lake near Buffalo, New York State (1996), shelters more than 5,000 seats with the use of only three internal compression members, which are also used to support lighting and acoustic equipment. The focus of the translucent membrane both in its form and in the lines generated by the cutting pattern is towards the stage area. The stagehouse is a simple, rectangular form clad externally in steel panelling with an interior, perforated-metal surface that reduces unwanted performance echoes and extraneous noise such as wind and rain. The lower portion of the walls is a curving, open-mesh fabric that stops 6 metres above the ground. This helps to merge the rectangular form of this part of the structure into the catenary membrane and reduces its visual mass.

FTL always endeavour to develop structure, engineering, lighting and acoustics strategies, simultaneously, as the design theme for each project progresses. The Sawyer Point Performance Pavilion, on the Cincinnati riverfront, integrates curving land-form structures into an acoustic reflective band shell with the public address system incorporated into the two symmetrical masts. Structure, enclosure, acoustics, performance technology and landscape, developed with the local firm Glaser Associates, have all been integrated into the overall form of the design.

FTL frequently act as consultants providing design, engineering, pattern-making, construction and manufacture-monitoring services to other designers who require specialist advice on tensile structures. One such project was for a *brise-soleil* for the new Central Library in Phoenix, Arizona (the building was designed by a local architect, Will Bruder). In this case the practical objective was to provide low-energy control of solar-heat gain and to protect the internal space from direct sunlight. From such pragmatic requirements a beautiful sculptural installation of diaphanous open-mesh shading devices has been created.[8] It not only reflects external light in the daytime but filters internal light at night. FTL have also used tensile structures to mitigate the hostile environments of existing buildings and to create settings that are more responsive to human needs. Their brief for the Bradford Exchange Office, Chicago (1985), was to create an entirely new environment within a large, open-plan office space. The structure was an enclosed shed, which the client wished to inject with a more relaxed natural atmosphere. FTL designed a complex matrix of tension structures, which have been suspended from the roof in a variety of patterns, to provide a soft, layered effect diffusing the light from banks of fluorescent fittings and roof lights. Careful modelling of all the panels, both to decide form and structure but also to test translucency percentages and ultimate lighting levels, was undertaken. The completed design utilised living plants and running water to create a remarkable interior environment.

Nicholas Goldsmith and Todd Dalland believe that tensile architecture is yet to realise its full potential.[9] If architects and engineers can gain control to the same extent that they have with structures which depend on compressive and bending forces, they will then be able to develop entirely new building forms that have a legitimate place in the architectural mainstream. Only then will the technological developments, which will no doubt continue to appear, be capable of being fully exploited. One such experimental form that FTL has investigated is the concept of tensile-membrane-clad skyscrapers. Multi-layered composite membranes, prestressed in tension, are the most efficient and most lightweight cladding medium and in this concept have been used to contribute to the structural rigidity of framed structures as well as providing an environmentally variable envelope.

Tensile architecture is not yet fully recognised as real building. It is more generally perceived as a useful medium for temporary shelter. Modern techniques can produce membranes that have a guaranteed life of up to thirty years – as long as many so-called permanent building materials. However, during the time it is in existence, the impact of a building on its users is just as important if it lasts for thirty days as if it lasts for thirty years. Sometimes membranes have been replaced to extend the structure's life in its original form, as in the National Symphony Orchestra Acoustical Shell in Washington, DC (1979). Sometimes the initial structure has proven the viability of the solution and the building has been redesigned and rebuilt in a manner more appropriate to a longer life span, such as in the Baltimore Pier Six Concert Pavilion. The work of this practice focuses attention on a particular structural strategy that has remarkable potential for a society that is becoming increasingly accustomed to change. Flexible living and working arrangements demand flexible building solutions that respond to changes without waste. This is obviously a concern for architects and engineers, however, it should not be perceived as a problem but an opportunity. FTL have shown that beautiful lightweight buildings can be made for the kinetic society of today, which have as much meaning now as the beautiful heavyweight buildings of the past had in their own time.

Procter & Gamble Pavilion at Sawyer Point, Cincinnati, 1986

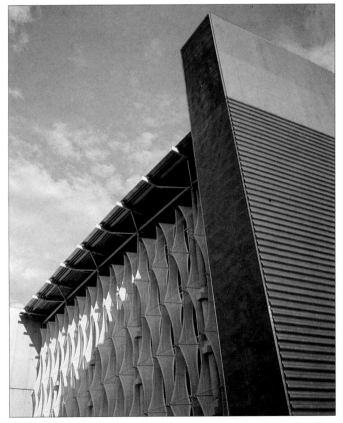

Sunshades act as *brise-soleil* against the summer sun on the north wall of the Phoenix Central Library, 1995

PIER SIX CONCERT PAVILIONS
Baltimore, 1981 and 1991

A particular phenomenon of temporary buildings is that if they are successful they often become permanent. This project began as a temporary performance structure, which was only intended to be erected for five years; it was based on a pier in Baltimore's inner harbour on land designated, in the long term, for housing. FTL's collaboration with another architect on this project led to a crab-like tensile canopy that provided a stage area and sheltered seating for 2,000 people with service and supporting accommodation in rented trailers and containers. The facility proved so popular that it was retained for ten years until the end of the fabric replacement period. FTL were then approached to design a larger, more sophisticated building with permanent support facilities that would, however, still retain the cost effectiveness and imagery of the previous tensile structure. The new building was to have a life span of at least fifteen years.

The inner harbour area had developed significantly in the intervening years – the concert pavilion being a major contributor to this renaissance. The new building – this time designed in its entirety by FTL –

responds to its improved surroundings with a structure that is both more formal and more graceful. The organic form of the vinyl-coated polyester membrane is a link with its predecessor, though this time it is organised into a series of regular bays supported by delicate masts and restrained by cables that meet the ground with the minimum impact. The tethering of the fabric skin is raised from the ground by concrete perimeter piers to provide the height for the building's users as they access it, but also to seemingly weight the relatively light 'sail' into place. The support buildings are simple geometric masonry shapes reminiscent of functional, harbour-side buildings, though their roofs also possess double-curved surfaces of standing seam metal that respond to the membrane surfaces that soar above. The new building can now seat 3,500 people under cover with a further 1,000 in sight of the stage on an external, terraced grass area. The internal acoustics have been designed by Jaffe, Holden, Scarborough and use both the reflective surfaces of the fabric and amplification equipment to modify the sound quality.

The intention of the brief for the original Pier Six Concert Pavilion was to create an image for the city in the manner of the Sydney Opera House, though on an incredibly slim budget. The earlier building consolidated the potential for the function of a performance facility on the site and also realised the desire for a dramatic identifiable form on Baltimore's waterfront area. For the new building, Todd Dalland exploited the drama and excitement of function and site further and indicates that tensile forms through their unique ephemeral character can contribute to urban settings in unsuspected and valuable ways.

FTL's original smaller pavilion in a parking lot, 1981

Pavilion seating plan

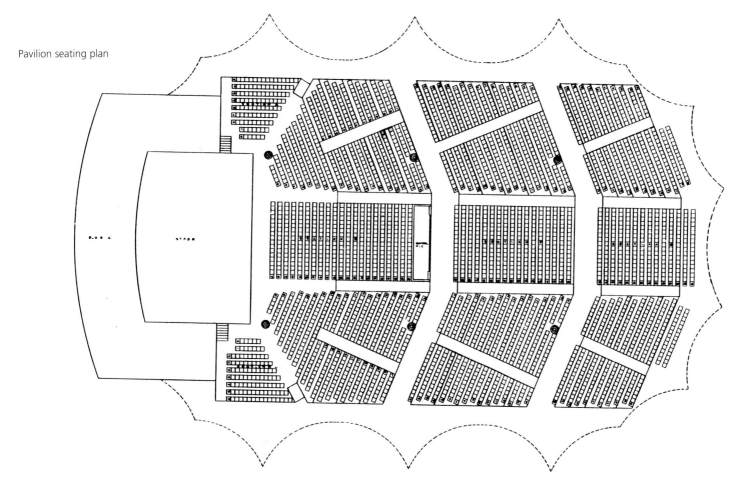

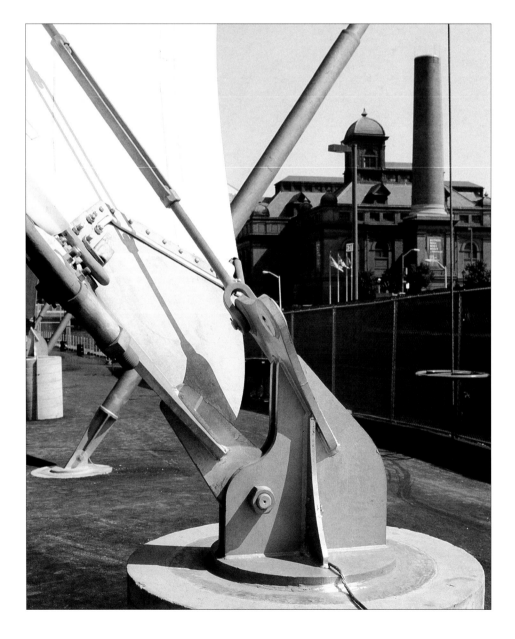

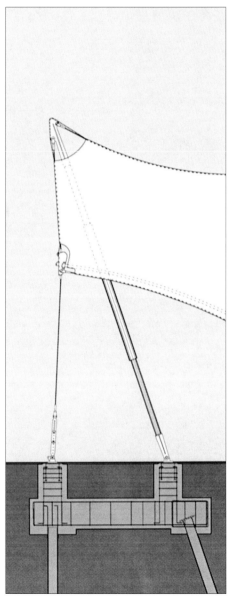

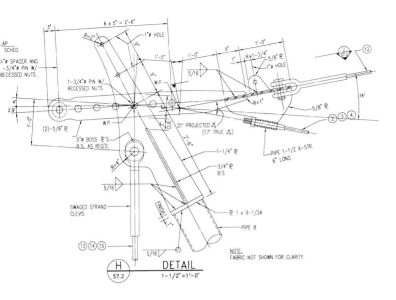

Edge mast detail

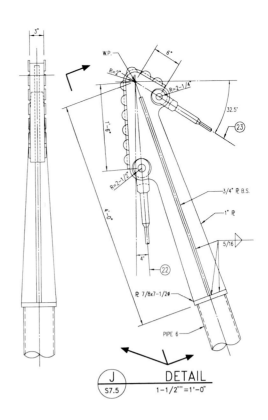

Edge mast at front pavilions

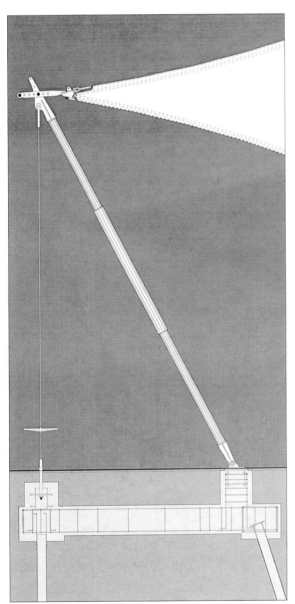

Edge mast at main pavilion

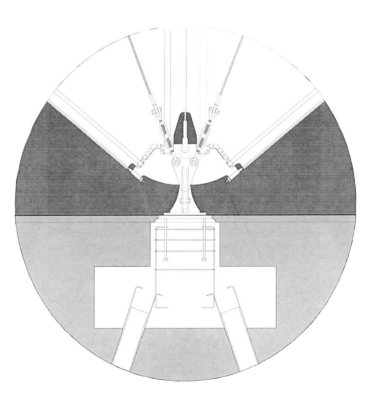

Valley detail

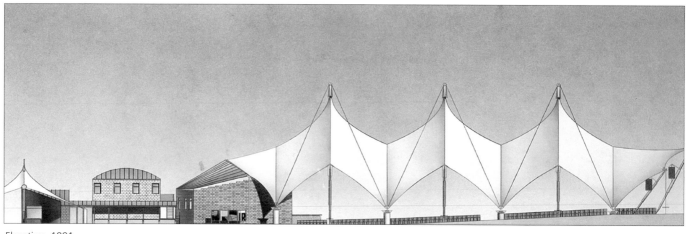

Elevation, 1991

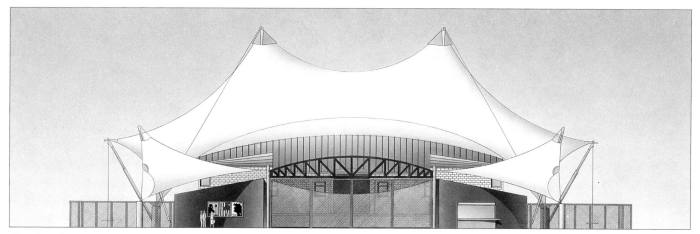

Elevation of entrance, 1991

FINNISH CHANCERY WALKWAY CANOPY
Washington, DC, 1993

The early experience of Todd Dalland and Nicholas Goldsmith was as designer/craftsmen/contractors directly involved in all aspects of the realisation of their designs. As their projects became larger and more complex this could no longer be possible, partly because of their scale but also because building-industry specialists had now emerged who were able to fulfil the constructional role effectively and economically. However, the desire for the most intimate involvement with the building process still exists within the practice. One recent project, where FTL have taken on a more integrated role in the manufacture of a structure, has been in the creation of a canopy over an elevated walkway at the Finnish Chancery in Washington, DC.

Finnish architects Heikkinen-Komonen were approached to provide a design concept to shelter a concrete platform that projects out into the woods behind the framed steel and glass façade of the main building. In response to the restricted budget and limited size of this project, FTL offered to act as contractor, as well as collaborating on engineering development, construction drawings and specifications. The resulting structure consists of an ephemeral floating membrane that follows the path of the walkway and oscillates up and down along its length. Only one vertical compression member is used for each panel, stiffness being obtained by cable stays radiating away from the structure to the woodland floor below. A repetitive rhythm is established by the panels and their associated triangulated booms. These members help reinforce an imagery reminiscent of yacht structures, though not overtly so – the main impression being of delicacy and balance. Most remarkably, the new structure, small though it is, acts as a delicate yet dramatic foil to the sharp-edged, crystalline form of the main building.

DEJUR AVIARY AT THE BRONX ZOO
New York, 1997

The Dejur Aviary at the Bronx Zoo had been in existence for more than a hundred years, when in the early spring of 1995 the old building dramatically collapsed as its steel-pipe structure (which had rusted from the inside) failed under the weight of an unusually heavy snow fall. FTL were approached by the Wildlife Conservation Society of the zoo to design a new aviary, which though it would be based on the existing site, would be 30 per cent bigger, more interesting to visitors, and more conducive to the requirements of its permanent inhabitants – the birds.

In order to maintain historic continuity and make the most of existing features, much of the old false rock work was incorporated into the new design as were the mature dense trees that surrounded the site. The 3,000-square-metre building is situated within a sinuous, concrete perimeter wall that in parts is submerged below ground, though it emerges at each end to accommodate cave-like entrances. These are important design features that maintain the illusion, despite the enclosing mesh, of a completely uninhibited external environment. The achievement of this design requirement has been assisted by the specification of an extremely fine 1-millimetre-diameter wire rope which has been woven into a 25-millimetre grid – at a distance this cable net becomes invisible to the visitor.

Though the new building is both visually and environmentally transparent, it must be able to resist snow loads, which can still gather on the mesh, and wind loads, though this is significantly less than for a comparable sized membrane structure. The net is supported by 300-millimetre-diameter steel arches, two of which spring from a single base forming a diagonal pattern on plan. The net acts in unison with the supporting arches utilising double-curved shapes to provide a rigid structural system. Though the building is symmetrical in section, its structure transfers visually from one side of the site to the other, creating an organic continuity that cannot immediately be understood, but which is still clearly resolved. Nicholas Goldsmith likens this to the patterns seen in nature. Such complex systems are harmonious, yet somehow also mysterious, in that they operate in symbiotic relationships whose interdependence is apparent though its meaning remains obscure.

Model

Aerial view

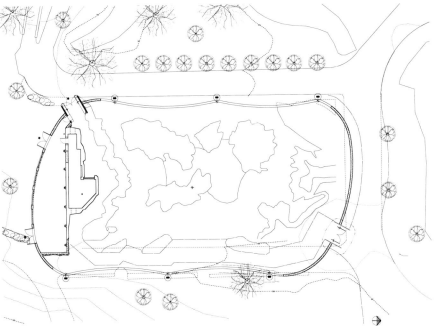

Site plan

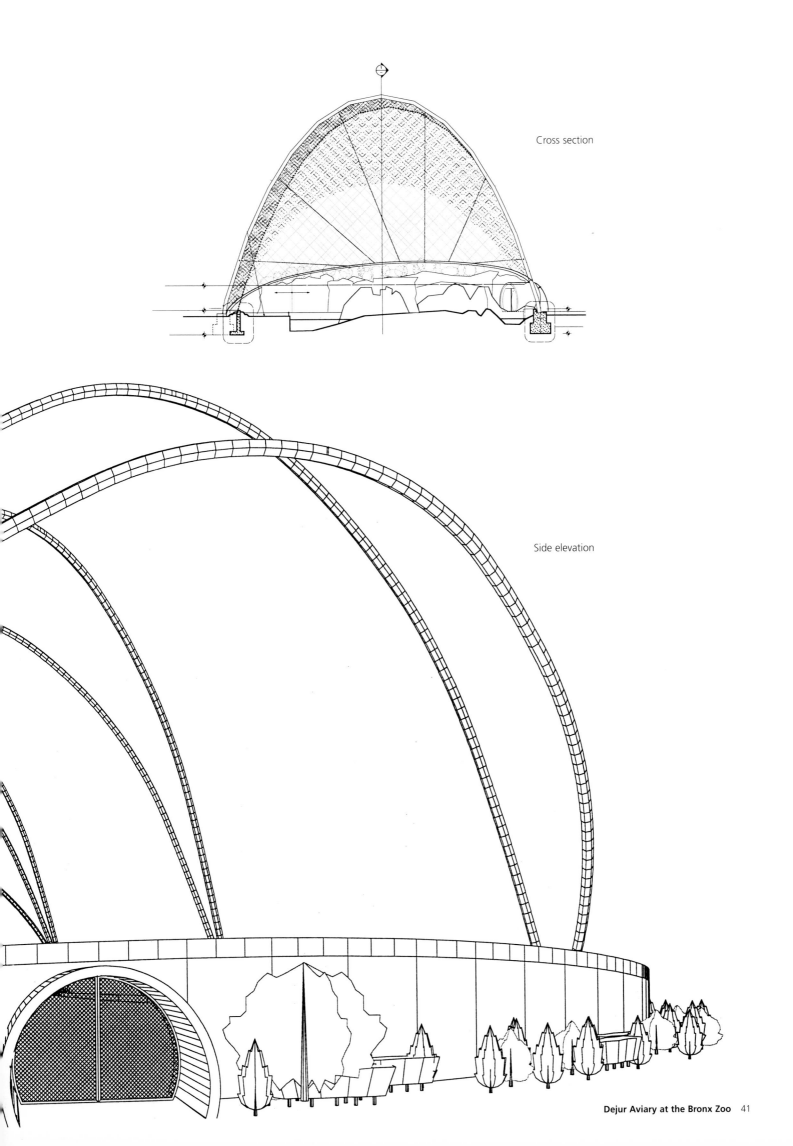

Cross section

Side elevation

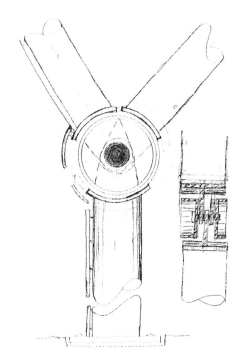

Initial concept sketch detail of intersecting arches

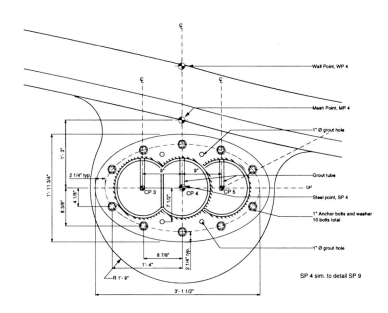

Plan detail of arch base

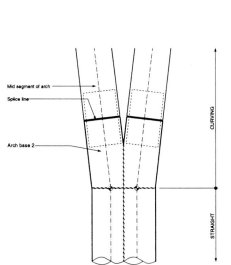

Elevation detail of mid segment of arch base

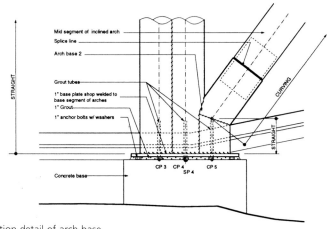

Elevation detail of arch base

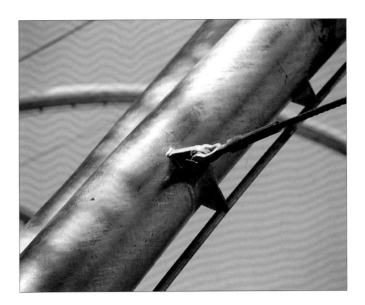

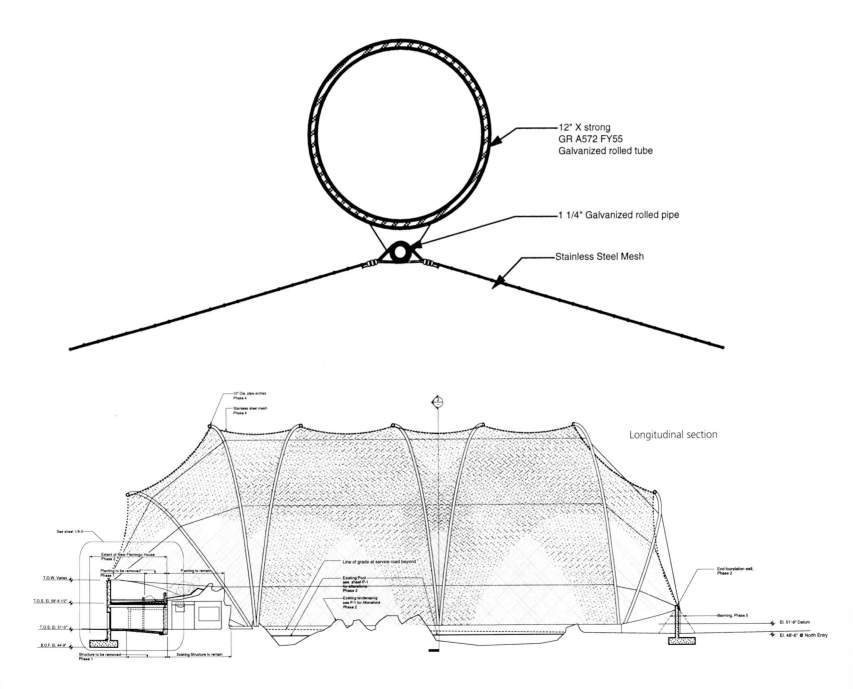

12" X strong
GR A572 FY55
Galvanized rolled tube

1 1/4" Galvanized rolled pipe

Stainless Steel Mesh

Longitudinal section

10" Dia. pipe arches
Phase 4

Stainless steel mesh
Phase 4

See sheet 1/A-5

Extent of New Flamingo House
Phase 2

Planting to be removed
Phase 1

Planting to remain

Line of grade at service road beyond

End foundation wall,
Phase 2

T.O.W. Varies

Existing Pool
see sheet P-1
for alterations
Phase 2

T.O.S. El. 58'-6 1/2"

Existing landscaping
see P-1 for Alterations
Phase 2

Berming, Phase 5

T.O.S. El. 51'-0"

El. 51'-9" Datum

El. 48'-6" @ North Entry

B.O.F. El. 44'-9"

Structure to be removed
Phase 1

Existing Structure to remain

BOSTON HARBORLIGHTS PAVILION
1994

The Boston Harborlights Pavilion represents many of the advantages of tensile-membrane buildings within a single design – a design which also strives to emphasise the aesthetic capabilities of this constructional strategy. The project was created for the commercial promoter Don Law as a seasonal, multipurpose-performance amphitheatre seating 4,500 people under cover. Although the initial intention was for the amphitheatre to accommodate music events, the structure has been designed so that a great range of other performances can take place including those in the round such as theatre, circus and sports. This flexibility is more and more frequently demanded by current operators in their efforts to avoid 'dark days' when the facility is not in use.

The building is only in operation during the high season, from spring to autumn. Making it demountable in the off season means that a more economic structure can be adopted, one which does not have to accommodate snow loads. It also affords the possibility of creating a completely portable canopy, which can not only be dismantled and stored, but can also be taken to a new location for re-erection.

The building has a number of features that relate to this specific requirement. The masts are all based in hollow sand pots (cylindrical, below-grade cast-concrete tubes which sit on piles), which enable them to be lowered or raised by adding or removing sand from the foundation. This allows the pre-stressed loads to be fine-tuned *in situ* without requiring complex equipment. The structure is also stabilised by a permanent 'guy web' system that enables the fabric to be removed without affecting the integrity of the supporting structure.

One of the main innovations of this pavilion has arisen out of the search for the most economic solution, though it has also resulted in a remarkable harmony of form. Wherever possible efforts have been made to utilise standard components and increase repetition – the most cost-effective way to manufacture complex structures such as this. The designers, Dalland and engineering partner/mentor Ian Liddell, have responded to these restrictions by creating a symmetrical structural form of great beauty. The main canopy consists of six geometric double-curved elements, each of which are in turn constructed of two identical opposing fabric panels. Each element is supported at the apex by a single, box-truss mast and at the perimeter by alternate tall and short columns. A second series of open-mesh tensile structures around the perimeter are tucked under the main fabric roof to help control the wind and the rain.

The entire architectural form is based in tension and compression on these six degrees of symmetry. The designers' response to the finger of land on which the building is sited is appropriately formal: visible from all sides, its crown-like shell possesses the same profile regardless of where it is viewed from the shore. The perimeter membrane is high enough to allow the audience to have views of the dramatic Boston Harbor sky-line, and its overall form ascends and descends, apparently echoing the rhythms of the music within.

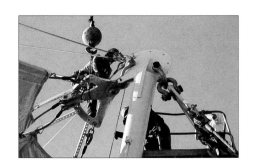

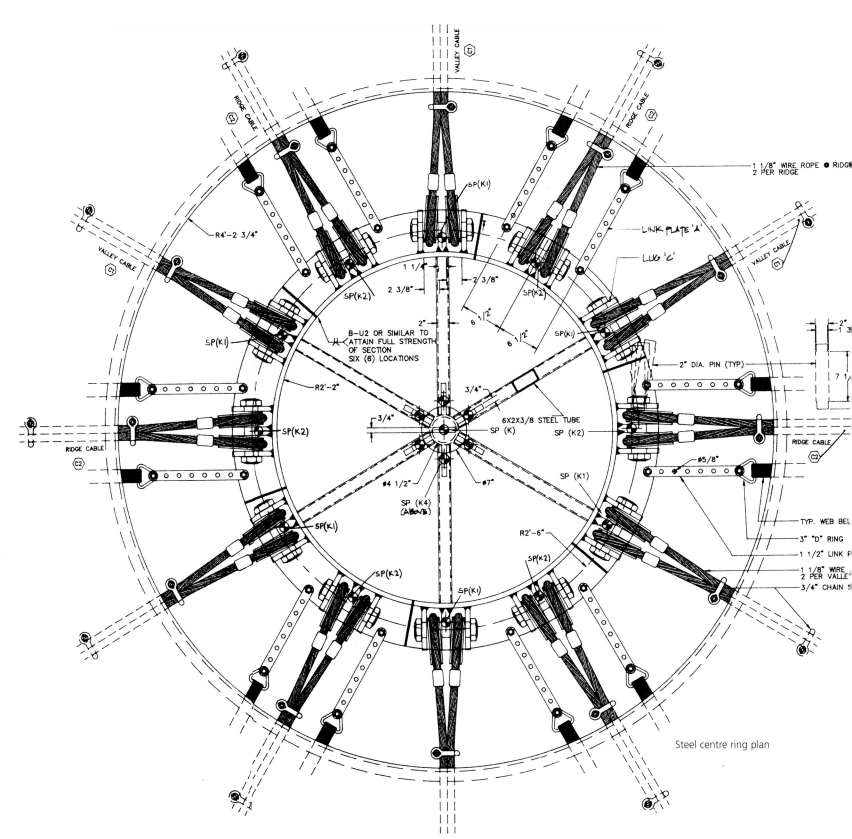

VALLEY CABLE C1

RIDGE CABLE C2

1 1/8" WIRE ROPE ⊙ RIDG
2 PER RIDGE

SP(K1)

R4'-2 3/4"

LINK PLATE 'A'

LUG 'C'

VALLEY CABLE C1

SP(K2)

1 1/4"

2 3/8"

SP(K2)

6 1/2"

VALLEY CABLE C1

SP(K1)

SP(K1)

B-U2 OR SIMILAR TO
ATTAIN FULL STRENGTH
OF SECTION
SIX (6) LOCATIONS

2"

6 1/2"

SP(K1)

2" DIA. PIN (TYP)

7 1

R2'-2"

3/4"

6X2X3/8 STEEL TUBE

RIDGE CABLE C2

SP(K2)

3/4"

SP (K)

SP (K2)

RIDGE CABLE C2

#4 1/2"

#7"

SP (K1)

ø5/8"

SP(K4)
(ABOVE)

SP(K1)

R2'-6"

TYP. WEB BEL

3" "D" RING

1 1/2" LINK P

SP(K2)

SP(K2)

SP(K1)

1 1/8" WIRE
2 PER VALLE

3/4" CHAIN S

Steel centre ring plan

Movement
EVENT SPACE
PORTABLE WORK
Robert Kronenburg

Everything in the circus is pushing beyond the limit ... Yet within this apparent free wheeling license, we find a discipline which is almost unbelievable ... The layout of the circus under canvas is more like the plan of the Acropolis than anything else; it is a beautiful organic arrangement established by the boss canvas man and the lot boss ... The concept of appropriateness, this 'how-it-should-be-ness' has equal value in the circus, in the making of a work of art, and in science.
Charles Eames[1]

Portable buildings have been in existence since humankind first began to build and yet it is only recently that they have begun to be recognised as architecture.[2] The general recognition that traditional forms of architecture are appropriate precedents for present-day designers who are concerned with building in a sensitive and ecological manner has also led to an examination of the portable structures which have been in use for millennia. The simply, yet elegantly, made buildings express their function in a subtle and harmonious manner that deals with pragmatic concerns of materiality, construction and structure, but also more complex issues relating to society and culture. Architects such as FTL who are developing a new genre of transportable buildings can therefore be shown to be working within a recognisable cultural tradition, though for many this may not be immediately apparent as it has been obscured by the complexities of recent history.

Most of FTL's work in this area can most accurately be described as deployable architecture, that is it consists of buildings of a precise, defined form that can be partially or wholly dismantled for easy transportation. Other forms of transportable buildings are: modular buildings that can be assembled in a number of different ways, utilising a kit of standardised parts; and portable buildings, which are transported in a fully or nearly fully assembled form.[3] FTL's work in designing modular buildings has been largely restricted to products for the standard tent-rental industry, though it has had a dramatic influence there.

Deployable buildings can be used for every sort of function as static buildings – large and small, simple and complex. Buildings for dwelling, commerce, industry, education, medicine and military use are common, though the most dramatic form of portable buildings are usually constructed for entertainment and as event structures – an area where the work of FTL has been especially influential. The size and operational characteristics of these buildings are impressive – and they are required to move as well! During the twentieth century the design boundaries of this type of structure have been significantly enlarged, proving Buckminster Fuller's assertion that 'building can be made to do much more than it could before'.[4]

From their very earliest projects Todd Dalland and Nicholas Goldsmith have been involved in the design of temporary and transportable event structures. Sometimes they have been movable only in order to allow them to be dismantled during the winter; in other cases the possibility of transportation to different geographic locations has been an important part of the design brief from the beginning. A wide variety of portable structure types have also been explored. The material for the United Nations World Population Fund Exhibition (1994) on international demography was prepared in New York, though the exhibition was to begin in Cairo at a dedicated conference.[5] The design team's response was to use the transportation crate itself as a module for the exhibition stands, which would be completely self-contained with all exhibition material, lighting and audiovisual equipment. Each of the eight rectangular aluminium-framed crates are mounted on wheels with the back-lit exhibition material protected behind wooden panels. Erection takes minutes: on reaching the destination the wooden panels fold up and are held in a suspended position by cables from a central mast extended from within the crate. Tensile-fabric panels are then stretched below the panels to create a sense of space around each exhibit.

The Carlos Moseley Music Pavilion (1991) is one of the most dramatic mobile structures ever made. The design brief was to make an instantly recognisable focus for classical music events that could be used on parkland sites in urban areas to encourage the maximum number of people to attend the performance. A wide range of technical problems were associated with its function – organisational, strategic, economic and acoustic. Commercial mobile outdoor-performance venues are, in their traditional forms, limited in size and crude in assembly techniques, requiring large numbers of assembly personnel and taking a considerable time to erect. For this project it was decided to create a new structure that could be erected in the minimum amount of time and as automatically as possible. In addition it was resolved that the quality of the performance should not suffer greatly, despite being outside the usual acoustic environment of the auditorium. Inspired by mobile-crane technology, Nicholas Goldsmith designed a distinctive pyramid structure that could be erected using readily available hydraulic systems. By converting standard flat-bed trailers, they created a portable foundation and stage area. A combination of an acoustically reflective, tensile-membrane orchestra cover and sophisticated portable amplification equipment designed by Jaffe Acoustics was used to provide a simulation of concert-hall acoustics. Though a wide range of complex problem-solving issues were dealt with the result is more than a response to the individual difficulties encountered. The image of the structure is genuinely as a piece of architecture, though it is of a new form that has its basis in movement rather than stasis.

FTL have used the Carlos Moseley Music Pavilion experience as a design generator for other mobile buildings, such as the Cadillac Exceleration Center (1995) and the Time for Peace Pavilion (1994). The idea for this mobile museum was created by artists Marion and Robert Einbeck and is intended to be a travelling harbinger for peace containing a wide range of interactive displays, events and performances on five stages within a single transportable structure. The building is based on eight trailer beds in which all the components are stored for transportation; they also form an important part of the assembled building. The structure consists of a single, symmetrical-tented volume based on the plan of a cross. It has been made purposefully monumental in its organisation and form, in order to symbolise the solemnity of the task for which it has been created. The central volume is the highest, its membrane

United Nations World Population Fund Exhibition, 1994

An event for Maurice Biederman at the 7th Regiment Armory, Biederman Gala, New York, 1983

Biederman Gala

suspended from four twin-compression members that are held in equilibrium by forces from the four minor membranes over the smaller spaces. The building owes nothing to traditional large-volume fabric enclosures, such as circus tents, as it both focuses the internal spaces into something more than just a shelter and it uses structure to generate a distinctive external image, a dramatic crown-like form, which is balanced and harmonious, yet dramatic and exciting.

A major theme of FTL's work is the creation of buildings that integrate structure and skin into a complete architectural form that is envelope, environmental modifier, and constructional and structural strategy all in one. This has particular benefits for mobile buildings which are more quickly operational if systems are integrated together. This integrated-design strategy requires much more care to be taken in the coordination of the different building systems, which in a conventional building are normally accommodated using standardised methods. Portable buildings cannot always rely on water mains and drainage hook-ups, power supplies may have to be from mobile generating systems, and simple infrastructural requirements such as hard standing for vehicle access may not be available. At the design-input stage, FTL promote the inclusion of specialist contractors who often have relevant expertise in these situations. The design of mobile buildings is not just about the creation of the physical elements of the building fabric but also about the logistics of its erection and dismantling. A structure that can be erected in six hours may be much more versatile than one that takes twenty-four hours to be assembled. The capital cost of the incorporation of additional automatic systems, however, may be much higher and must therefore be carefully evaluated against the advantage of the requirement for less site-erection personnel.

Costing of static buildings has in the past been primarily directed towards capital cost. This is now changing as the effects of energy usage and operational expenses are calculated at the outset of building design to provide a more accurate life-cycle cost for the project. Portable buildings work very well in this scenario as they do not have to be serviced when they are in a dismantled state; site costs are negligible and the value that the operator receives from the building can often be very much greater. A portable building can be geographically situated where it will be most effective and the people who are to use the building do not have to travel far to reach it. Its operator can also be totally in control of how a dedicated facility is used and avoid situations which are outside his control when renting an existing building. Some of FTL's promoter clients are now having their own venues built because they can use them for a wide range of events, and when they are not in use they do not have to maintain a costly empty space. They can also make additional profits by controlling their own catering and sales venues and by

taking the show to the exact location required to target the maximum audience, irrespective of availability of appropriate performance spaces. These are the pragmatic economic benefits of operating a dedicated facility as opposed to fitting events into rented, loose-fit, permanent structures. Promoters such as this are not initially interested in the architectural form which is generated, as much as the ease and cost of erection and dismantling. This leads the designers to create pragmatic solutions where the deployment engineering is operational and reliable on a repetitive basis. However, the drama of tensile-architectural forms, which is intimately connected with their structural integrity, means that even the most simple, efficient tensile membrane has an inherent beauty. This feature is not lost on promoters, who also wish to create the best possible show by attracting performers to use their venue and the paying public to attend the event.

In the past, the perception of standard portable buildings has usually been poor. Temporary has been synonymous with disposable: standard products that have been selected primarily on the issue of price. The real potential of portable building is that it is reusable and flexible, valuable features in today's prevailing environment of continuous change. Todd Dalland's involvement with the tent-rental industry has undoubtedly led to the availability of better standard products. These have not only been of value in conventional standard deployment situations but also flexible enough to be used as the core component in special situations to which have been added unique, specially designed elements that provide individuality and character dedicated to the event. The Seventh on 6th Fashion Village shows (1993) and Olympic Games (1996) facilities are examples of this strategy.

The creation of dedicated portable-building projects produces potent images of a kind of architecture that has not existed before: an architecture that is based on lightness and minimal materials – dynamic structures that have a specific purpose which is recognisable in their form. Static long-life, loose-fit buildings are part of every urban environment in the world, however, they do not contribute to the recognisable specific identity of different communities. The technology of portable structures possesses lessons for those involved in the design of static ones and forecasts a more flexible, responsive built environment. They use minimal materials and components that can be deployed in different ways to meet changing site and operational conditions. They provide a medium for the enhancement of transfer technology as they are responsive to the employment of elements that have been developed for other purposes in other industries. All the portable structures designed by FTL have been prefabricated in workshops and factories using details that have been influenced by systems already used in truck, boat and aircraft manufacture. Portability in architectural design is a response to a specific logistical component in its brief, and it should therefore be viewed as part of mainstream architectural development. This is not only because it can and often does fulfil the same functions as found in static buildings, but also because its benefits become more easily transferable if it is not viewed as something outside the ordinary. Portable architecture has the potential to change dramatically the way in which the building process is viewed, from something static that responds solely to long-term requirements, in a relatively inflexible way, to something that provides dedicated solutions to needs of indeterminate duration – a type of building that can be altered, reused, reformatted to provide dedicated solutions again as uses and demands change. FTL's work in this field is among the most advanced in the world and the strategies they have devised indicate models for future development.

A series of aluminium trusses create an enclosed relocatable theatre environment, Bill Graham Traveling Ice Show

A kit of tensile architectural elements are used to create performance spaces, World Financial Center Winter Garden Performance Structures, New York City, 1987

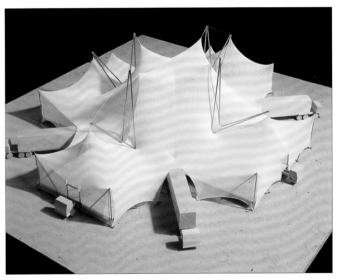

A deployable museum showcasing the growth of peace throughout the world, Time for Peace Traveling Pavilion, 1994

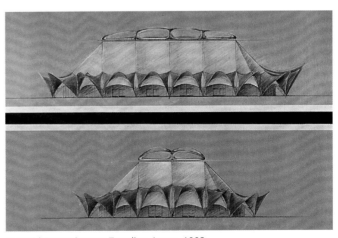

Pyramid Entertainment Traveling Arena, 1993

SEVENTH ON 6TH FASHION VILLAGE
New York, 1993 to present

Transient architecture has the power to transform the way in which specific locations and environments are both used and perceived. For those who have seen it in its new role, a site that has been adopted and adapted in a new way can never be quite the same as it was before. New York's Manhattan Island has one of the world's most unique urban settings, a densely packed infrastructure that has somehow maintained a pattern of distinctly defined neighbourhoods, so powerful in their separate characters that they can almost be described as villages. The concept of creating a new 'neighbourhood' for a specific purpose arose from the desire by the Council of Fashion Designers of America to organise a unified event for their biannual autumn and spring fashion shows, which were traditionally held in designers' showrooms around the city. As well as conventional architectural and interior design consultants on this project, FTL also served as theatre designers and event coordinators – tasks usually undertaken by specialist production and stage-set companies. Utilising standard commercial products from the range of Anchor Industries' tents designed by

Todd Dalland, a complex pattern of interlinked external and internal spaces was created in Bryant Park, a small green space behind New York City Library. Three main catwalk auditoria were assembled, the largest containing nearly a thousand seats, together with a wide variety of sales spaces and supporting storage, changing, communications, servicing and catering facilities. Though standard products were used, the efficient tensile patterning of the Dalland-designed structures provided soft forms that harmonised with the designer clothes, which formed the main focus of the venue. Free-form tensile structures were used both internally to provide dramatic backdrops to the auditoria interiors and externally to signal site entrances. The semi-translucent forms are particularly dramatic at night when the internal lighting is transmitted through the skin of the building, providing floating emphemeral reflections of the events within.

The Seventh on 6th event has been repeated several times. Though the basic pattern has remained, each time the facility has been reconstituted the opportunity has been taken to develop it further both technically

and organisationally. In this way, it is different from traditional portable performance structures such as circus tents in that its re-erection has resulted in incremental improvements – a constant developmental process is under way as lessons are learnt and utilised to improve the next deployment. Some special items at early shows have now become standard features, and the standard items, tested repetitively, can now be improved in efficiency. On an urban level, each time that this 'neighbourhood' is erected it stimulates anticipation and memory in the city's inhabitants and reinforces the concept that architecture can be flexible and ephemeral, as well as solid and permanent.

Elevation of Bryant Park to the rear of New York City Library

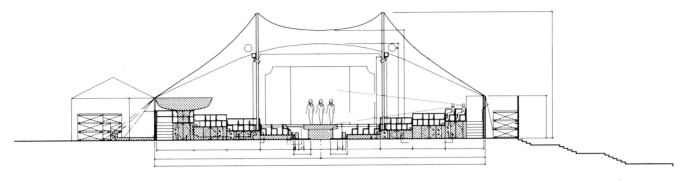

Cross section of Gertrude Pavilion, 1996

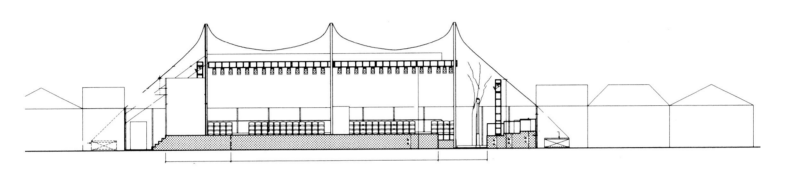

Long section of Josephine Pavilion, 1996

Part site plan of Josephine Pavilion, 1996

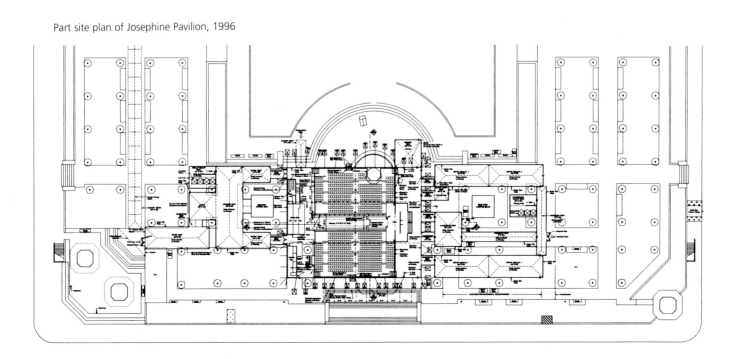

CARLOS MOSELEY MUSIC PAVILION
New York, 1991

It is rare that a truly new architectural form emerges, especially when the basis for its design results directly from function. Though portable structures have existed for thousands of years, it is only in the late twentieth century that the provision for outdoor events has led to new logistical building systems that are by necessity synthesised with the performance technology that they use. It could be argued that structures which do not incorporate any enclosed spaces are not buildings as such. In the case of the Carlos Moseley Music Pavilion, however, there is no doubting its architectural presence. Though the form of the structure has been developed to respond to a brief that requires a performance pavilion which can be erected in a wide variety of sites in just a few hours, its image is without doubt a response to the need to establish an identifiable venue, promote the excitement and anticipation for the event to come, and to heighten the quality and communication of the performance.

Designed to enable the Metropolitan Opera and the New York Philharmonic to undertake an annual series of summer performances in New York's city parks, Nicholas Goldsmith developed the structure with the specific fragile locations of the city's green spaces in mind; however, its portability and flexibility enable it be used in any location accessible by normal roads. The entire facility is transported on six standard semi-trailers (articulated lorries) which provide a mobile base for the structure. Once on site, three of the trailers form the foundations for a hydraulic, self-erecting tripod structure from which a taut, translucent fabric shell is deployed. This acts as a sound reflector for the music and also as a screen for the computerised lighting system and video projection. At night the tripod structure disappears completely and leaves the image of a dramatic sail-like form surrounding the performers. The stage is folded like an accordion for transportation and is erected by hydraulic rams on to a frame of aluminium beams, also supported on truck-trailer beds. The complex acoustic performance created inside a concert hall is reproduced by a unique portable sound system developed by Jaffe, Holden, Scarborough. Sound from the stage is picked up by microphones and is mixed in a special mobile booth and then transmitted by radio to twenty-four battery-powered loudspeakers dispersed at carefully graduated distances from the stage. The acousticians have calculated the infinitesimal time delays that are required to produce the concert hall sound, and these are programmed into the reproduction system to give the impression of the reverberation that is so important to classical music. The structure has now been in use for six seasons and has proven its value not only for its original purpose but also for special performances with additional customised equipment.

This structure blurs the distinction between building and machine. It clearly has an architectural character when deployed; however, its repetitive erection process has resulted in a constructional strategy that relies on automatic and semi-automatic systems. The structure is therefore operated rather than erected. Its success lies not only in the utilisation of mechanical systems to make architecture but also in the fact that these systems do not overshadow the architectural character that they generate.

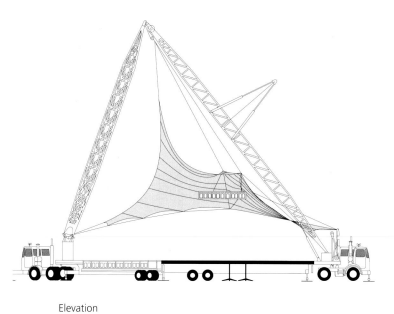

Elevation

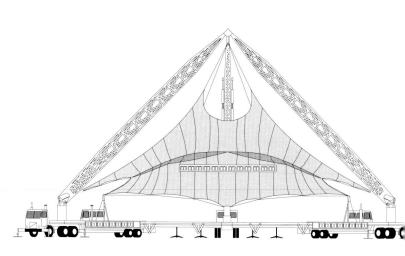

Elevation

Deployment sequence of facility

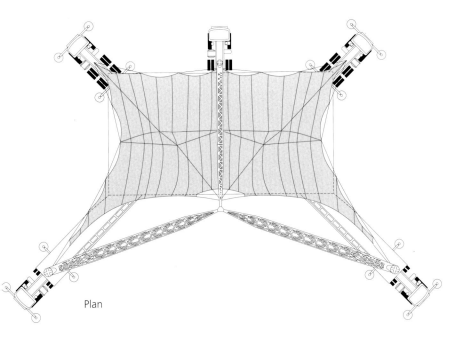

Plan

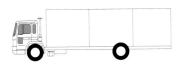

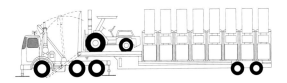

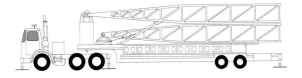

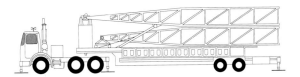

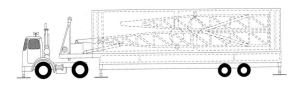

The truck fleet

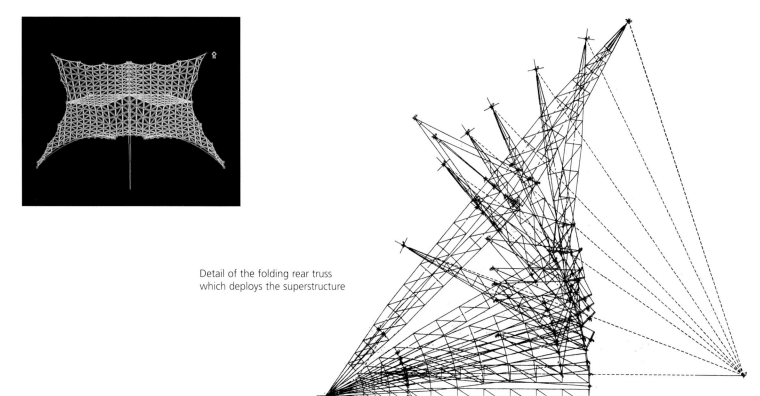

Detail of the folding rear truss
which deploys the superstructure

Detail of aluminium membrane clamp plate

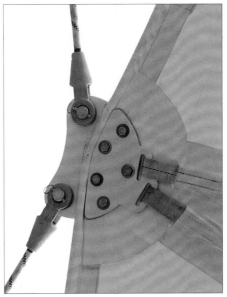

Detail of ridge with kevlar rope assembly

Model

CADILLAC EXCELERATION CENTER
West and East Coasts, and Atlanta,1995

The Cadillac Exceleration Center project can be seen as a development by Nicholas Goldsmith of the Carlos Moseley Music Pavilion concept. Though it also depends for its structural strategy on a tensile-fabric skin supported by a tripod, it is paradoxically both more simple and more complex than its predecessor. It is simpler in that a less generous budget resulted in an erection procedure that did not rely on relatively sophisticated hydraulic systems, and more complex in that the brief required a completely enclosed space which would be capable of providing full blackout facilities for audiovisual presentations.

Two facilities have been made, one based on the East Coast and the other on the West Coast of the USA, though they were also deployed in Atlanta for use during the 1996 Olympic Games. Each consists of a travelling-theatre space seating approximately 125 people that, combined with more conventional commercial marquee-type structures containing seminar and catering facilities, form a mobile facility for training personnel involved in the sale and maintenance of Cadillac automobiles. The entire building is transported on two semitrailer trucks and consists primarily of three trusses which can be folded in half for transport; a conical fabric membrane; and a wide range of supporting technology, including power generators, air conditioning, lighting and audiovisual equipment.

The erection process can be completed in under twelve hours. The trusses are swung out to their full length and locked into position. Two trusses are fixed with helical anchors into the ground and together at their apex. The third is attached to the others at the apex and to a small flat-bed vehicle at the base via a special attachment. The apex is suspended from a crane, and as the base of the third truss is driven in towards the centre the apex of the tripod is lifted into position. When the correct geometry is reached the base is also fixed to the ground. The fabric is hoisted up by cables running through one of the trusses. Complex moving joints are required at the bases of the fixed trusses due to the rotational geometry they must pass through as the tripod tilts up to its final position.

The travelling components of the building are kept to a minimum as use is made of locally available, standard-rental equipment for the erection process. This has reduced its capital cost and transportation expenses. Despite this use of standard, locally available support systems, its dynamic form gives it a unique character which ensures that its presence signals the commencement of a special event – a valuable asset in the facility's role as a promotional and educational tool.

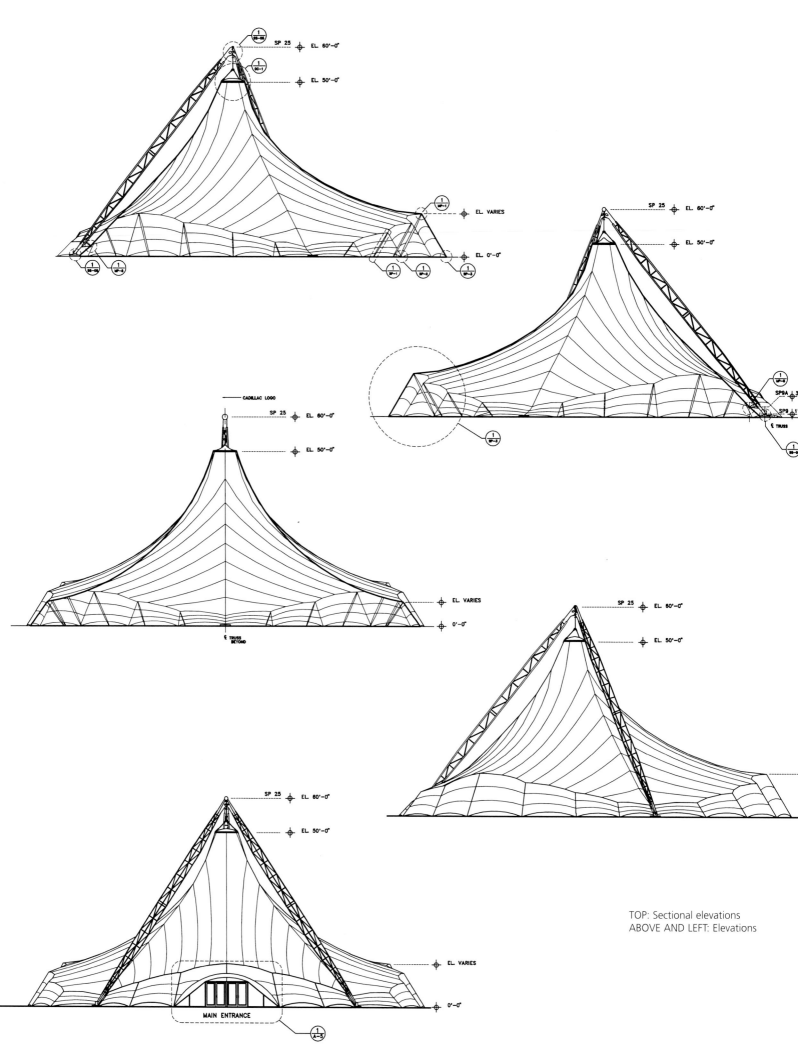

TOP: Sectional elevations
ABOVE AND LEFT: Elevations

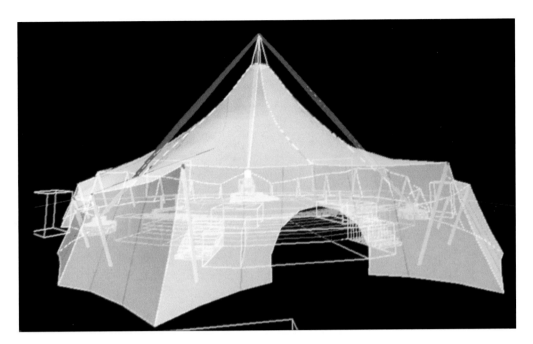

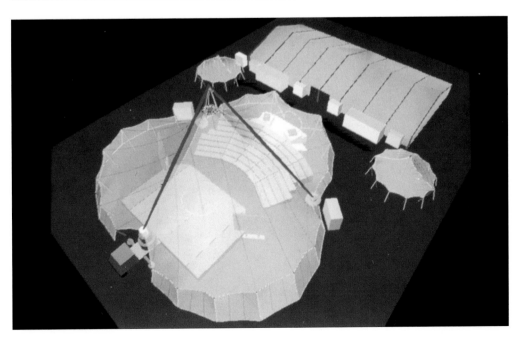

Computer
simulated drawings

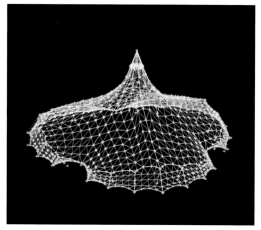

CAD rendering of the membrane

Gimbel detail

Partial deployment of facility

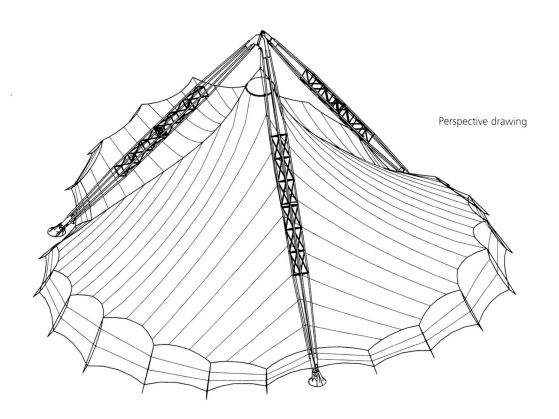

Perspective drawing

ATLANTA OLYMPIC GAMES 1996

Large international events have always demanded temporary facilities. Higher expectations and more complex strategic ambitions, however, have meant that recent events, such as the Olympic Games, require infrastructural arrangements that are equal in complexity to permanent urban layouts. City-sized roads, pedestrian routes and servicing arrangements are needed to cater for the vast complexes of temporary buildings, fulfilling all the functions found in a permanent urban neighbourhood. Despite the scale of the demands, facilities must be established in a remarkably short period and, if the project is to be both economically viable and ecologically aware, should not waste resources by being based in permanent buildings that will become redundant once the event is over.

The athletic venues and related amenities for the Atlanta Olympics were resourced in three ways: approximately a third was made up of existing local sports facilities; a second third was accommodated in new permanent constructions; and the final third (about 150,000 square metres) utilised temporary and relocatable buildings and interior adaptations. FTL was one of the key design firms involved in planning the temporary infrastructure of the 1996 Olympic Games at Atlanta. They

adopted several different roles during the design and implementation process: their work ranged from comprehensive organisational tasks, such as planning a range of temporary hospitality villages around the city, to specific construction projects, like engineering the 40-metre-tall 'pyramid' structures at the Athlete's Village. Todd Dalland's experience of organising large multifacility events, such as the Seventh on 6th Fashion Village shows at New York's Bryant Park, proved invaluable in determining the requirements of the Olympic Games' temporary infrastructure and in urban planning for it.

FTL were codesigners of the 'Look of the Games': a portable kit of parts, which was used in many of the forty separate venues as a unifying feature to help direct the hundreds of thousands of athletes and visitors. These urban-scale temporary structures were made from standard rentable items such as scaffolding with additional, specially designed modular elements, including printed-fabric panels, tensile membranes and above-ground concrete ballasting.

FTL were project architects for the 21-acre Olympic Centennial Park, which provided a focus in the heart of downtown Atlanta for all the athletes and visitors. This free facility attracted crowds of up to 250,000

people and contained several venues which were open to the public long into the night. The Centennial Park's major facility was the AT&T Global Olympic Village, a 9,000-square-metre complex, comprising three relocatable buildings, which included FTL's Cadillac Exceleration Centre. These buildings, designed in collaboration with Last Design Company, incorporated two-storey, movable-glass curtain walls, relocatable interior elevators and a second-storey bridge between buildings. This structure's fabric also became an entertainment effect in itself as images from Olympic events and live concerts were projected on to the outside of the building. AT&T plan to tour this facility, taking it first to Nagano, Japan, and then on to Sydney, Australia, for use at the Olympics in 2000.

This temporary city, enlivened by interactive communications and human activity, was constantly active during its limited life. An integral part of the design concept, however, was that it could then be dismantled and be reassembled in a different form at another geographical location. In this way, it is a potent realisation of the dreams of architectural activists of the sixties and a stimulating glimpse of what a future urban environment might be like.

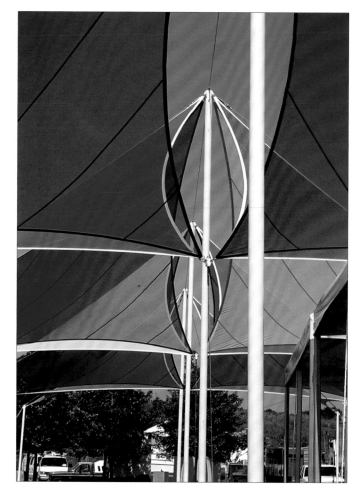

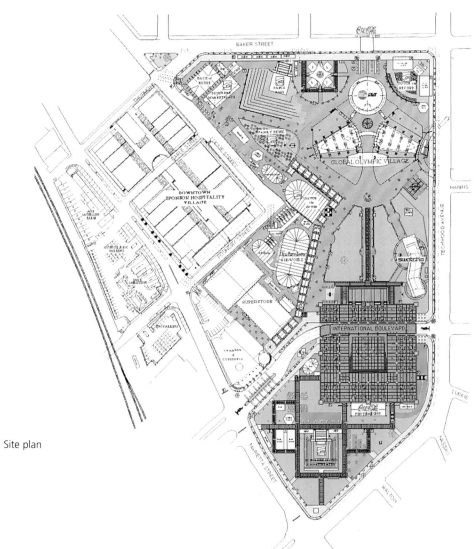

Site plan

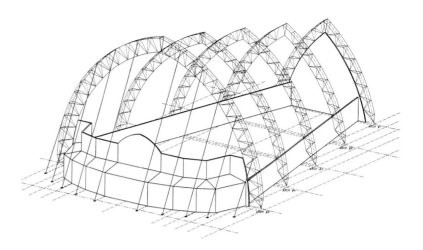

Light
SOFTNESS AND MOVEMENT
INTEGRATED WORK
Robert Kronenburg

The search for lightness (is) a reaction to the weight of living …
Italo Calvino[1]

Lightness has a double significance for tensile-membrane architecture. Both meanings of the word are related to it: lightness as weight, and lightness as illumination. The pursuit of the ultimate, lightweight architectural form could be seen simply as a search for an enclosure with the largest span that requires the minimum effort; however, though this adequately describes the pragmatic basis of this endeavour it ignores a range of ancillary factors. Minimum structure for maximum span describes economy, even efficiency. The real essence of the tensile membrane is that it appears to embody the antithesis of mass and its structural form is expressive of that desire. Stiffness is more difficult to achieve without mass, and lightweight structures are therefore generally more flexible than heavy-weight ones. They must, however, tolerate movement without it affecting their structural integrity. Such buildings do not have the inert appearance of their compressive, bending counterparts and can often be seen to respond to loads placed upon them by their inhabitants and by the atmosphere. This kinetic potential is fulfilled to the ultimate when the entire building is designed to be mobile – a feature that is a direct benefit of the characteristic light weight of the structure. Light structures also have a greater capacity to be manufactured with delicate members: the loads and forces with which they deal can be articulated in slender lines of material that provide visual clues to their direction and size. Compression members are dense and therefore usually opaque. However, careful design of their shape can indicate the points of transference of force and identify the areas in which they must resist bending. Cables and ropes that gather the forces in membranes are also opaque, as are the joints between the different mem-brane panels, which are clearly visible against the translu-cent material. These joints can all be positioned by the designer, and when placed with care and sensitivity they provide a visual reference to the way the forces in the structure are gathered and dispersed.[2]

Illuminated light affects the design of tensile-membrane structures in significant and remarkable ways. All architectural form is perceived through the medium of light, however, for most it is light which is reflected from a surface. In many cases this is also true for tensile membranes. Polyester-fabric membranes can be obtained in a standard range of fifteen to twenty colours and a completely opaque surface can also be specified for blackout situations. Fibreglass-based products and polyester can be obtained as translucent membranes with up to 20 per cent trans-mission of light. Though this does not sound much, in fact it provides an incredibly well-lit interior environment in which all usual visual activities can easily be undertaken. Even translucent fabrics appear opaque from the outside during daylight hours, and in this situation the visual image of the skin is soft and gently polished like an eggshell. It will frequently appear to take on the hue of the sky: bright on a summer's day, cool in overcast weather. Fabrics do not usually have conventional openings and the membrane when viewed from outside is a continuous skin that provides a homogeneity to the surface reflection.

Within the volumes created by translucent membranes a different form of light effect is generated, only seen elsewhere in completely glazed structures. In this situation the whole space seems to contain light in a way which it is not possible to duplicate with artificial lighting. This 'spatial' light is the closest that can be achieved to being outside, though being within a building the occupant is also able to experience controlled atmospheric and acoustic environmental conditions. In this situation the occupant also retains an awareness of the external conditions as changing outside light levels affect the internal environment.

At night, translucent fabrics communicate the internal, artificially lit environment which, depending on the situation, can be the warm glow of continuous interior illumination or the dynamic flickering lights of a performance. The surface can also be used for more literal communication. The AT&T Pavilion at the Atlanta Olympic Games (1996), for instance, featured the projection of images on to the outside and inside of the fabric. Such surfaces therefore offer far more opportunities in situations like this than conventional opaque building skins. FTL have also used the translucent quality of membranes to explore new ways of creating interior environments. The Bradford Exchange (1985) is a permanent installation that utilises membranes to provide a largely artificial environment with an external ambience. Membranes have also been used in temporary situations such as the Seventh on 6th Fashion Village shows (1993) and the Biederman show to create display effects, using both reflected and diffused light.[3]

FTL's more conventional architectural work began with the reputation they earned for working with such temporary environments. The fashion industry is obviously conscious of the characteristics of fabrics and the temporary events, which are an essential part of the fashion calendar, provided an appropriate vehicle for FTL's skills with fast-track, low-cost structures. This led to their involvement in projects for showrooms, design rooms and office interiors for specific designers. Frequently, this work involves developing interiors in which lighting is an important factor and their knowledge of the way that light can be used with fabric surfaces has been valuable. Both Todd Dalland and Nicholas Goldsmith have used the fashion-house work to explore the development of contemporary architecture, though in quite different manners. Dalland's Carmelo Pomodoro Showroom and Offices (1992) accepted the qualities of a typical loft floor without adulterating or concealing its existing surfaces, and then used movable objects to inhabit the space and order the environment. These objects were made from a range of materials that continued to explore the inherent properties of the double-curved surface, essential in tensile-membrane design. Goldsmith's DKNY Headquarters uses conventional materials throughout and sets about inhabiting the rooftops of the city. A completely glazed, glowing volume rests on top of a conventional office building. It mirrors the translucent qualities of the tensile structures used elsewhere within the building and also conveys the impression of light weight necessary in the creation of a structure that must rely on the foundations of its host. Though very different, both these projects exhibit an integrated approach to

'Tensil' lighting system fabric panel designed to eliminate glare in computer work stations for Sunar Hausermann Office installation, 1985

World Financial Center Ferry Terminal, New York, 1989

World Financial Center Ferry Terminal

building design that is born out of their experience with tensile-membrane structures. Each has been designed from an early stage using physical models (as are the fashion interiors and event structures) and each utilises materials in a way that exhibits consummate understanding: the DKNY Headquarters in its choice of differing materials to represent the familiar rooftop buildings of the city and the billboard hoarding that forms the glass house; and the Carmelo Pomodoro Showroom with its planar plywood surfaces that are a foil to the curving steel and fabric forms.

Despite these and other similar projects that use conventional materials, FTL's major work is tensile-membrane buildings. The sites for these buildings usually enable them to be viewed from all sides even though many are located within the city. The projects situated on the pier sites at Baltimore and Boston add a new perspective to the city edge: situated on water surrounded by hard, rectangular and usually much larger buildings. Even so, these buildings complement their environment and hold their own within it, their smaller size being balanced by the excitement and drama of their form. Major cities are recognised by their skyline and tensile structures are a definitive addition to any horizon. The nature of a building's use is also conveyed through its form and, like the Sydney Opera House, an identifiable public building in a prominent position makes a powerful statement about the city's relationship with its citizens. Portable buildings can also have a similar effect. The influence of temporary structures extends beyond the time during which they are in use because the memory of their impact on the site lingers on for those who experienced the event. This is especially so for structures like the Carlos Moseley Music Pavilion, which revisit the same venue year after year. Not only is there a memory of the way the space was when it was inhabited by the building, but there is also an anticipation of the event to come. Event structures like this are a physical, identifiable element that gathers groups of people together through a common experience – a communal event in a mutually responsible society. Permanent buildings can symbolise the continuity of society, the presence of history and confidence in the future. Portable buildings can also be permanent structures, though with temporary sites, that have the added benefit of immediacy and relevance. Of course, because they require renewed effort to be brought into fruition each time they are relocated, their existence is more tenuous. However, this also means that they are a clearly visible sign that a special effort has been made in their realisation, and it is all the more valuable for that.

The work of FTL is intrinsically interwoven with the major concerns of architectural thought today. Their projects are generally not those sponsored by rich organisations with limitless resources, but are built to strict budgets that dictate maximum value for money. In some cases this has been the main reason why the practice has been chosen as consultants. However, these economic ambitions are also about making 'less do more'. Using less materials to create a satisfactory solution is economically sound and is also ecologically aware, as it is using less of the world's resources both in raw materials and usually in manufacturing energy. Buildings that can be adapted for use in different ways are also more efficient and can be better tuned to any current changes in commercial and social conditions. FTL use technology as an inspiration in their designs; not in order to create an image but as a meaningful part of pragmatic though aesthetically considerate solutions. They are in control of the technology they use and have been at the forefront of its development. They have gained their knowledge both from working with the pioneers in the field but also from manufacturers, contractors and their own first-hand experience from twenty years' work and nearly a thousand individual design projects. As professionals, they are naturally concerned with the projects that they develop for their clients and have evolved design procedures that ensure satisfactory end results. However, as consultants to industry they also see the long-term view and have established criteria that will help develop the architectural medium in which they primarily work.

They believe it is their duty to promote tension structures as the most efficient constructional principle yet devised, though they still recognise the need for more efficient construction techniques in this field which would enable greater modularity and allow higher tolerances to optimise the design possibilities. They also know how important it is that the skills and knowledge of manufacturers, fabricators, maintenance servicers and operators are incorporated into the design process, though they add that it is the designers' duty to lead the building industry into better construction procedures and to encourage the introduction of new products and procedures. The architect's role should therefore not be one of a passive assembler of components but of a proactive instigator of new procedures that directly effect the way that buildings are created.

The tensile way of building utilises systems which cannot be anything other than they are, and it is therefore totally honest in the way that it describes and communicates the forces that are generated and controlled in its materials and components. To work within the strict rules, which this form of construction defines, requires that the designer be totally in control of his medium. If this is not the case, unresolved structural issues become clearly visible in the resultant design and the harmony and balance, which are such an essential component of these buildings, are conspicuously absent. The criteria and formulas necessary to create these forms can be learnt; however, some skills that are an indispensable part of the creative process can only be acquired by experience, particularly a working knowledge of three-dimensional aspects of form generation. A true awareness of the geometric shapes that make stable membrane shapes and how those shapes interlock to create useful and beautiful spaces is not something that can be discovered without actually taking a direct part in the design process, making mistakes and experiencing success. This is also a form of architecture that cannot be fully appreciated through illustrations. The complex volumes, patterns of light, the nature of air movement within a flexible membrane have to be directly experienced to be completely understood. Tensile architecture comes closer to humankind's natural inhabitable forms than anything so far created, and it does it in a manner that is not a copy of nature – for that would be fruitless – but in a way which focuses the essence of light, of balance and of organic form in a recognisably man-made system. Throughout history, sculptors and artists have taken nature as their subject in the hope that by exploring its visual form they will come to find out more about humankind's place on the Earth. What has been called organic architecture has had a less ambitious aim, though still a worthy one, to harmonise the environments which are created for human use with the world that surrounds them. It is possible that tensile architecture does something more than this: by expressing so clearly its relationship with weight and gravity, light and space, it contributes to our understanding of the spirit that we find in nature which makes it so important in our lives. There is no doubt that Nicholas Goldsmith and Todd Dalland show a deep awareness of these issues in the buildings they have created. Their work exhibits an intimate involvement with the generation of innovative architectural forms and a Utopian ambition that is inextricably linked with the potential of tensile architecture. Todd Dalland has described their work in this area as an attempt to blend technology and poetry; this suggests an approach to building that assimilates realism with spirit. Their method is to anticipate the changes that are occurring in the way people use buildings and to respond to them with the application of appropriate and efficient construction techniques based on design procedures developed from real experience.

'From where will a new architecture emerge?' is the question that began this exploration of FTL's work. Perhaps a sustained vision such as their's, which combines technology and poetry in the creation of evocative economical forms, is one area where the answer might be sought.

A relocatable building describing Solidere's development of downtown Beirut after the civil war. It was to be the first new building in the city. Beirut Exhibition Pavilion, Beirut, 1995

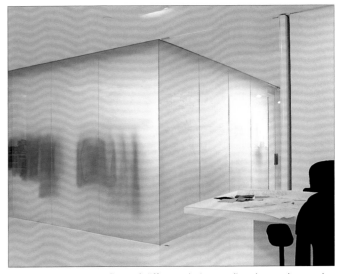

A 1,000-square-metre floor of different design studios clustered around a luminous glass conference room, Donna Karan's Design Studio, New York, 1990-96

Tension truss roof

CARMELO POMODORO OFFICES AND SHOWROOM
New York, 1992

Only rarely do client's desires and the designer's ambitions entirely coincide, though it is more common when both parties are directly involved in creative work. A prerequisite for this is a personal as well as a professional understanding. Such was the case between the late fashion-designer Carmelo Pomodoro and Todd Dalland.

Pomodoro's increasingly successful fashion house required new offices, a production unit and a showroom, which was to be fitted into a typical Seventh Avenue fashion loft in Manhattan. Dalland decided to expose and clean the existing building fabric to form a backdrop for an assemblage of introduced objects, all of which also expressed their materiality. The curved form, which expresses efficiency and strength in major structural roles, is here transposed into an interior design project and is utilised as a foil to the hard-edged functional background of the existing building, and as a harmonious constructional counterpoint to Pomodoros's clothes and fabrics which are the focus of the installation. The soft, gentle surfaces of fabric stretched on metal frames or from wire cables were used to reflect natural and artificial lighting.

Mill-finished steel followed similar double-curved forms. Only the plywood partitions, suspended and supported at orthogonal angles, reflected the planar surfaces of the existing structure. Standard galvanised piping (which also crisscrossed the ceiling space to form the sprinkler system for the existing building) was used to frame specific static items of furniture, such as the reception desk to which panels were fixed in a disjointed, part-assembled manner that gave the impression of work in progress.

The Dalland-designed tables were constructed from steel rods in complex linear patterns that also defined the chords of double-curved surfaces. Virtually all the fittings were designed to be movable, some of the heaviest steel objects were on built-in wheels enabling them to be pushed around the showroom floor. This enabled the six separate sales areas to be reconfigured into an open display and event space as required during the fashion season. After Pomodoro's tragic early death, the contents of his showroom were auctioned off and are now, perhaps appropriately, scattered throughout the fashion houses, offices and apartments of Manhattan.

Fashion-house work is by definition transient architecture. This project, however, further extends it to a developing language of authentic, movable architectural objects, which utilise materials in a way that begins to impart their essence – usually only achieved when such materials and constructional strategies are used in a strictly structural sense.

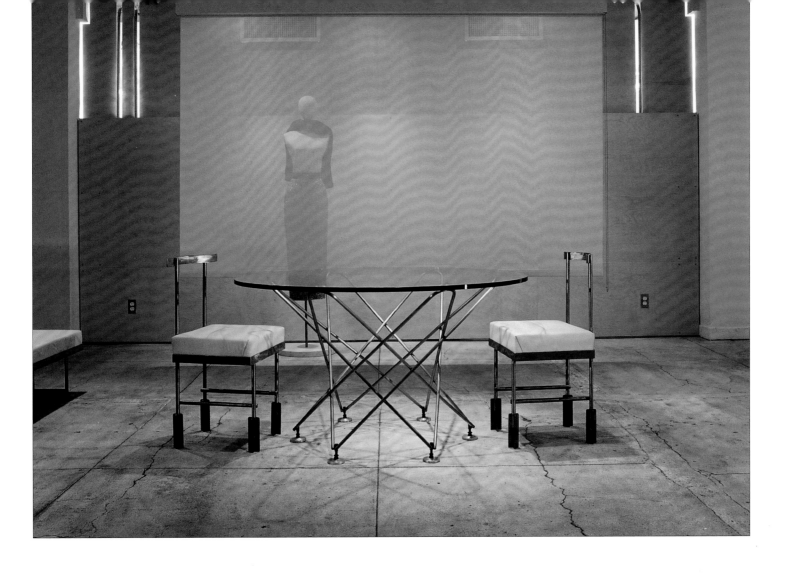

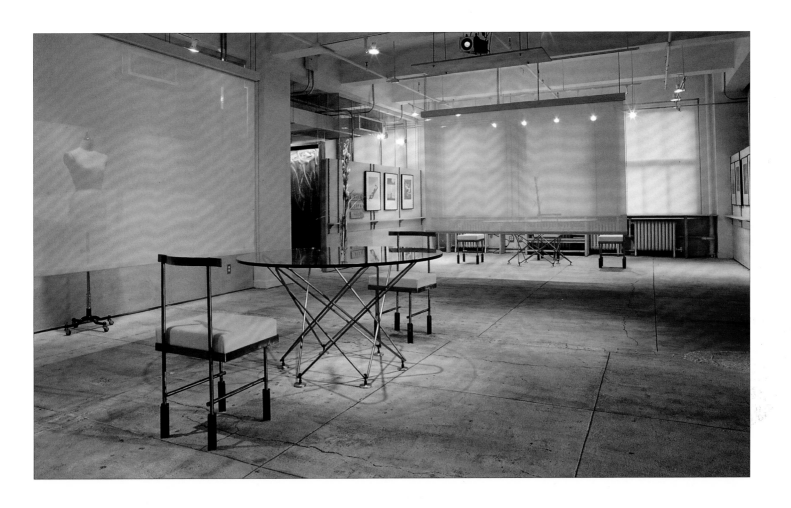

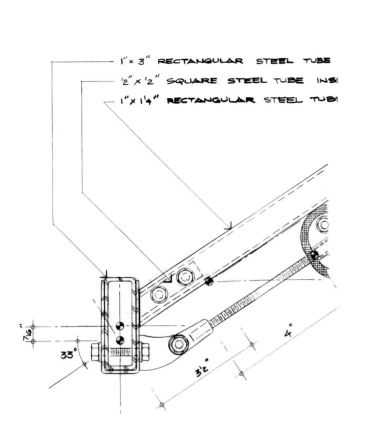

1" x 3" RECTANGULAR STEEL TUBE
½" x ½" SQUARE STEEL TUBE INS
1" x 1¼" RECTANGULAR STEEL TUB

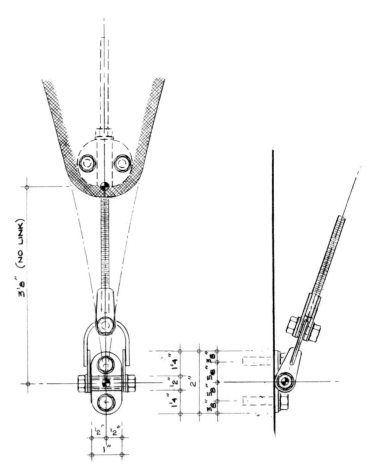

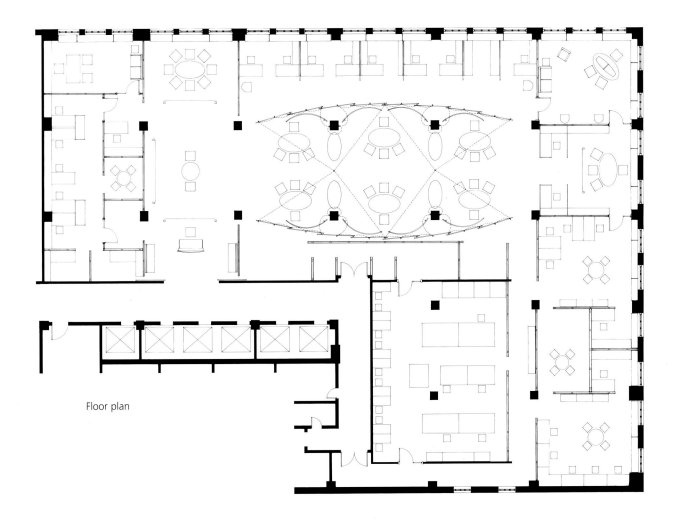

Floor plan

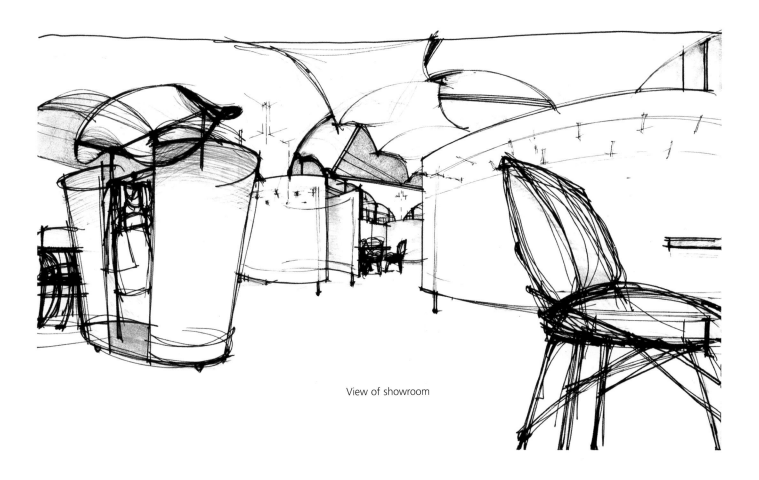

View of showroom

DKNY HEADQUARTERS
New York, 1990-96

The skyline of New York City, or more specifically that of Manhattan, is the most famous in the world. Fashion habitually adopts icons and transforms them for its own use. Donna Karan's Manhattan-based fashion house has done just that with the city, taking recognisable elements and utilising them in the image it has created for its clothes. However, not all the images are site specific: the generic North American rooftop scene of intermingling shapes – service structures, lift houses and water towers – is used, as is that most familiar, urban object, the billboard, which is most effectively adopted in the DKNY company logo.

DKNY occupy a twelve-storey 1920s building on a crossroads adjacent to Times Square. It is a building which has gradually been taken over by the company and converted by FTL so that ten floors have now been completely refurbished in a minimal architectural style; the concept is of a 'fashion laboratory' that expresses the designers' philosophy of an evolving style based on understated elegance. The ultimate built expression of DKNY's involvement with the city can be seen in their intention to occupy the roof of their building – up there amidst the everyday clutter of building services and advertising that forms the core of the company's image, as well as with the dramatic views of the canyons of the city, the Hudson River, and the skyscrapers that soar above the general matrix of downtown.

Though Nicholas Goldsmith's two-storey penthouse addition has a static building envelope, the flexibility required in its use has led to a dynamic interior. The key element is a barrel-vaulted, steel-framed, glazed volume that usually operates as a showroom, though with the aid of concealed pull-out bleacher seats it is converted into a catwalk space. It is during these events that the essence of the structure's purpose is most clearly understood, as the models parade against the backdrop of the Manhattan skyline. From the adjacent buildings this steel-framed structure has the presence of a large billboard, with most of the hoardings removed, except of course for the DKNY logo. The other newly constructed elements that surround the 'hoarding' inhabit the roof like a group of functional service shelters made from different materials such as masonry, steel and glass block. A dramatic circular stairway, linking the upper and lower floors, allows the showroom visitor to step out of the building completely to temporarily become part of the city.

Though the penthouse adopts and adapts to the city environment and clearly merges into its scenery, it can also be seen as a sort of symbiotic structure: its function supported by the workrooms and offices in the building below. It is therefore a transparent expression of its purpose, appropriately at the apex, or head of the structure. Glowing and symbolic capitals on tall buildings are a tradition apparent in the best examples of New York architecture – for a building that houses a fashion house, the idea of the head emerging from the clothes seems an entirely appropriate expression of that contained within.

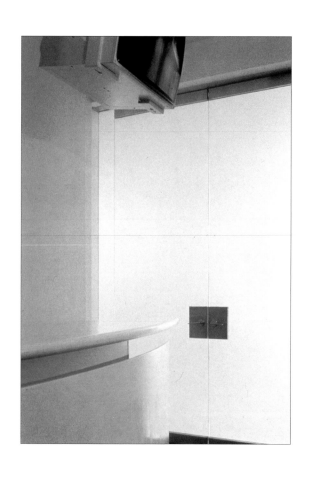

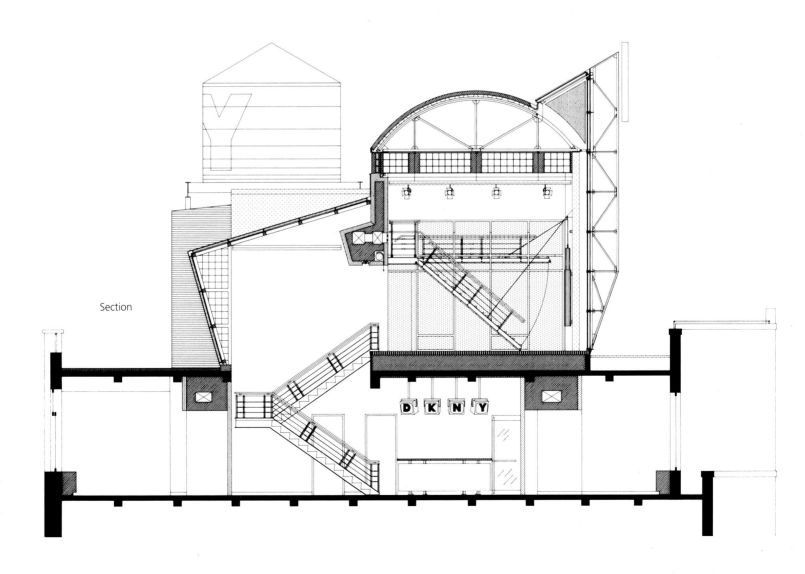

Section

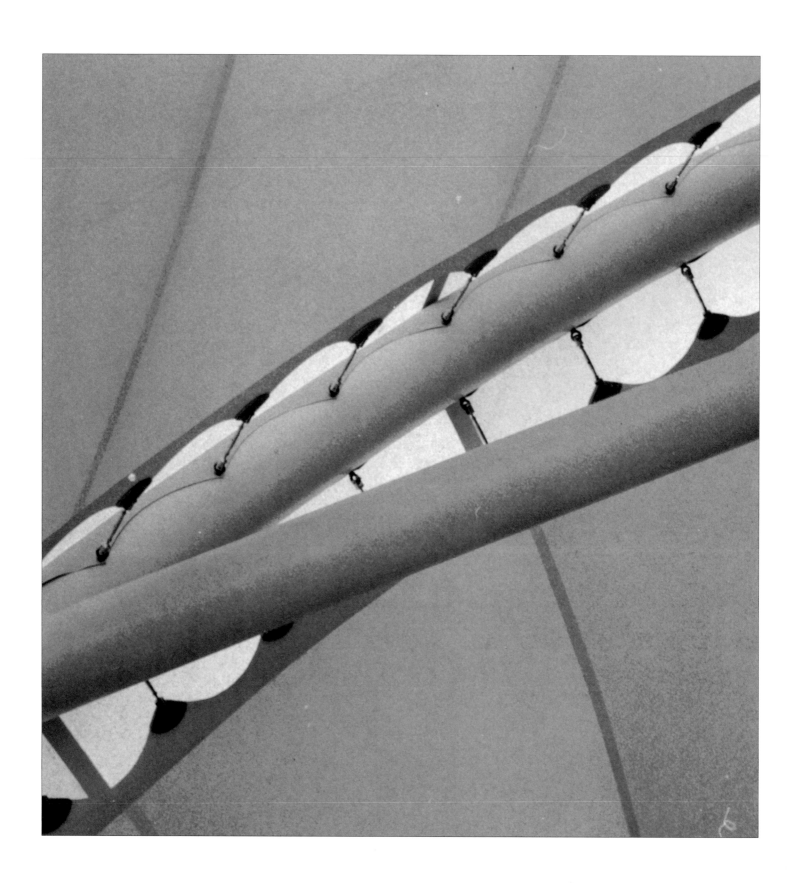

MOMRA PENTHOUSE
Riyadh, Saudia Arabia, 1994

Though the siting and cultural demands for the design of this project could hardly be more different from the DKNY Headquarters in New York City, the concept of the symbiotic building is taken further in this recreation centre situated on the roof of the six-storey Ministry of Municipal and Rural Affairs in Riyadh. The brief was to provide space for staff leisure activities at a new urban government building, though zoning regulations required that any additional structure should not be seen from street level. Nicholas Goldsmith consciously sought to provide a dramatically different environment from that of the building below in order to encourage the facility's users to acknowledge the change from their demanding working environment to one dedicated to recreation. An organic plan beneath a soft, tensile, Teflon-coated fibreglass membrane was therefore designed to counterpoint the orthogonal plan and rigid envelope of the existing structure. It is significant that once the designers had made this decision to create a refuge, isolated as far as possible from its host in form and sub-stance, they chose to prepare all their presentation models and drawings as independent images, representing the top of the building as a site plan rather than an existing structure.

Though it uses sophisticated modern materials the building form refers to the traditional tent dwellings of the region, both in its use of a soft, tensile form and in the gathering together of functions below a continuous undulating sheltering roof. The internal environment is open plan between each of the activity zones allowing the twin-skin roof, supported on steel, tree-like arch structures, to flow freely throughout the whole building. The separation between outside and inside is dematerialised by the positioning of the continuous glass skin, which shelters beneath the edge of the membrane and crosses the floor, paved in natural, sand-coloured local stone.

The requirement to be invisible from the street has been turned into an advantage, as from within the building the city below disappears and the view is of the sky and the horizon. Though the new facility relies on the building beneath it for its function and physical support, it has completely rejected its formal qualities. This radical contradiction to the existing building mass contributes to the creation of the dream-like quality of the new structure, a feature that is accentuated by its animistic form, which suggests a gigantic winged creature that has momentarily settled on the roof. This image must surely contribute to the feeling of escape for those who temporarily shelter in its shadow; the analogy with lightness and movement is also highly appropriate for a structure that relies on another building's foundations.

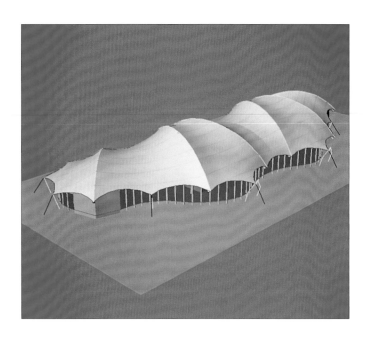

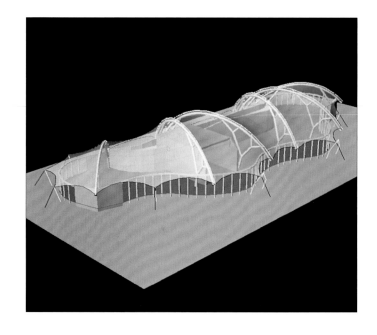

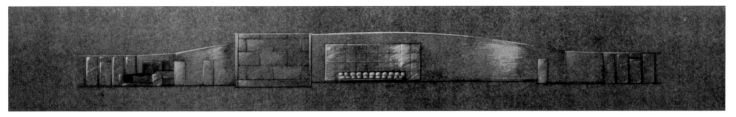

Elevation

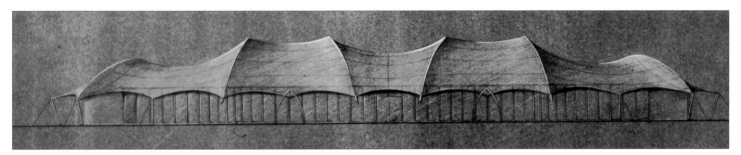

Elevation

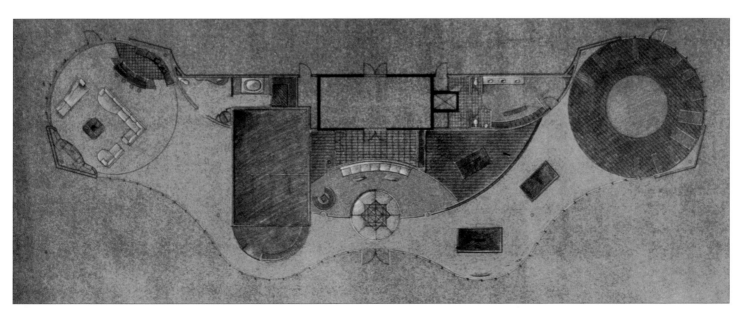

Plan

Oval clamp tensions, fabric tear-drop opening to lighting stem

STATEN ISLAND ESPLANADE
New York, 1996

Surrounding Manhattan there is more than fifty miles of waterfront bordered by land that has traditionally been used for commercial activities associated with shipping and waterways maintenance. Like every port in the world, New York has seen a shift in the way its harbour facilities operate, with more emphasis being placed on containerisation (there are vast container terminals in New Jersey) and air freight. This has meant that there are now opportunities to redevelop this area, comparatively little of which has been available for public access, despite its open views to Manhattan. One major location where redevelopment has begun is St George, Staten Island, to which the famous Staten Island ferry crosses from Battery Park, Manhattan. The greatest views of the city's tip can be seen from the ferry, yet the Staten Island terminal makes little provision for local or tourist pedestrian traffic. As part of the programme for making the waterfront areas of Staten Island more attractive for new mixed-use residential and commercial development, the New York City Economic Development Corporation invited the landscape-architects Johansson and Walcavage

to redesign the area with a special focus on public use. FTL were appointed as artist/architect/engineers for one of two special sculptural projects on the pedestrian esplanade leading to the ferry terminal.

Todd Dalland employed FTL's usual method for developing a concept of making physical models. These were then used to present the design to New York City Arts Council, who reviewed the projects for the NYEDC. Dalland's idea was to provide a sheltered space from which pedestrians could view Brooklyn, Manhattan and the Verrazano Narrows Bridge. Though the sculptural concept began as a grove of metal and fabric trees, there are obvious visual connections with the bridge; although it is several miles away, it is an important element on the skyline conveying the image of a beautiful tensile sculpture rather than that of a functional object. The design works within the structural limitations of the ramp upon which it is sited, which could only accommodate small point loads without bending or lateral stresses. The appropriate structural solution for a shelter in this situation was simple portal frames and Dalland has taken

this strategy and dramatically reworked it. The 'trunk' of each 'tree' explodes into a helical expanding mesh of 'branches' – 15-millimetre-diameter stainless-steel rods that collect into a rectangular frame at the top. Each tree is counterbalanced by its mirror image to form the arch (and the portal frame) which is then repeated along the esplanade to create an avenue. The connection details from the 'trunk' to the 'branches' and the deck are made out of sight so that the structures communicate the purity of their form. An illuminated fabric membrane fits within the branches, however, it is interesting that in this case the double-curved shape of the taut membrane is echoed by the stainless-steel rods whose beauty exceeds that of the fabric. However, the fabric is an essential part of the overall concept as it not only provides the shelter element in the design, it also provides an illumination surface that enables the sculpture to vary remarkably in character between day and nightime.

POSTSCRIPT

Over the past few years we have taken a journey which has essentially been divided into three parts: first, a period of learning through apprenticeship, university and real life experiences; second, a start in professional life characterised by an aversion to the normal methodologies, and an attraction to the *Zeitgeist* of the late sixties and early seventies, and their revolution-ary approaches applied to building; third, the creation of a mature architectural and engineering practice whose emphasis lies in the development of special structures as a desire to expand architectural vocabularies.

All the above, however, is well documented in the body of this book. So where do we go from here? What has twenty years of designing tensile structures prepared us for? Thinking back to being children, we remember reading booklets about the year 2000 with its colonies on the moon and exploration to other planets and celestial architecture. One only needs to see the Kubrick film *2001* again to realise how naive we were and how slowly our built environment actually changes. The brave new architecture that was bursting out of the ruins of societal life after the Second World War has been so severely constrained (especially in the United States), that architects in general are responsible for a continually diminishing impact on the built environment. The explosive growth of American construction during the past fifty years is one primarily of strips, malls and themed residential architecture, be it federal, Tudor or ranch.

At the same time, the past few years have witnessed an explosion of digital images that are excelerating so fast we find it hard to keep up. Architecture is presently a medium of stone, concrete, wood, steel and glass. As such, it is always behind the styles and latest visual of the moment. As the acceptance of these images quickens, the man-made built world becomes further and further out of touch. There is no other industry today which has moved so slowly in accepting its technical development as architecture. Maybe we need to rethink our concept of architecture, to create a method of building that can respond to the effervescent explosion of technology surrounding us. Maybe building façades should be projected images, changing whenever necessary. Maybe buildings do not need to be designed for the millennia, some buildings need only last five years, others fifteen years, some possibly one hundred years and still others one day. Why do we design all these buildings with the same materials? We don't have to. If we as architects cannot or choose not to respond to the notion of change in our buildings, we only exacerbate the problem of our relevance as a profession.

Our work addresses these questions of duration and flexibility: structures that range from the temporal to the permanent, buildings that constantly change. It is interesting to know that the definition of flexible is: capable of being adapted, modified or moulded; characterised by plasticity; pliant; responsive to meet the requirements of changing conditions. In aeronautics, flexible means nonrigid. So by definition, the very notion of flexibility is linked with the material aspects of nonrigidity.

Let us look at buildings which will require this flexibility in the next millennium: museums and galleries, especially those which show media art; sports venues which are based on event marketing; schools where population shifts require growth facilities for short periods of time; and travelling performance venues.

Almost as a throw back to primitive times, architecture has once again become a shell – a basic shelter or a skin to contain an everchanging interior environment – a biological structure much like ourselves. If the traditions of architecture drew inspiration from the funerary structures of ancient Egypt, the future will be one which draws from the nomadic tents of the peripatetic civilisations.

Todd Dalland and Nicholas Goldsmith, March 1997

NOTES

Introduction

1 Frei Otto refers here to himself and Ted Happold. From 'Oration, 1st July 1996, at the Memorial Meeting for Worship at the Friends' House in London'. Reprinted in Eve Matthew and Thomas Happold, *In Memorium*.

2 Otto is widely acknowledged as the most important pioneer in the development of lightweight structures. In a series of projects from 1955 onwards he created innovative buildings that utilised tensile-membranes, tension nets and compression shells as an integral component of their design and organisation.

3 Bernard Rudofsky, Paul Oliver and Amos Rapoport have brought about a realisation of the important role that nonprofessionally designed buildings have had in shaping the built environment as a whole. See Bernard Rudofsky, *Architecture without Architects*, Museum of Modern Art (New York), 1965; Paul Oliver, *Shelter Sign and Symbol*, Barrie and Jenkins (London), 1975; Amos Rapoport, *House Form and Culture*, Prentice Hall (New Jersey), 1969.

4 Banham stated that architects lost control to such an extent that it blinded their awareness of the possiblities of new structural materials: 'If light-weight buildings, however, appropriate on all other counts, were poor insulators, the call was not for better insulation, but for heavy-weight structures in traditional masonry.' Reyner Banham, *The Architecture of the Well-Tempered Environment*, 2nd edition, University of Chicago Press (Chicago), 1984.

5 Reyner Banham explored this aspect of the Modern Movement in his influential first book *Theory and Design in the First Machine Age*, Architectural Press (London), 1960, and Martin Pawley reiterated and updated many of his observations in his sequel *Theory and Design in the Second Machine Age*, Basil Blackwell (Oxford), 1990.

6 *Shelter*, Shelter Publications (Bolinas, California), 1973.

7 The installation was erected by Larry Medlin.

8 Philip Drew, *Frei Otto: Form and Structure*, Crosby Lockwood Stopes (London), 1976.

9 The concert shell was, infamously, featured in the local newspaper after a student riot at a Deep Purple concert. The Preston Thomas Memorial, made from Dacron fabric and steel cables, was the group's first permanent structure.

10 Ian Liddell and Eddie Pugh joined Happold to form the core of a lightweight structures unit.

11 At the meeting, acoustician Chris Jaffe was intrigued by the idea of a tensile structure and was influential in the decision to award the project to the young designers. This structure continues to be used to this day and is set up three to four times a year.

12 Dalland comments that the idea of 'future' architecture remains extremely important to the firm, and that, paradoxically, it is not hard for those involved with contemporary technology to make 'future' buildings, as society in general is so slow to adopt new ideas that even old concepts still appear 'new' (in conversation with the author, December 1996). Jan Kaplicky, co-founder of Future Systems' confirms this view as he has repeatedly stated that his practice uses materials and techniques which have already been tested in other industries and, though they are often used in fresh situations, are not new at all (in conversation with the author, November 1994).

13 *Tensyl-XM* is currently under development with Buro Happold. It is an enhanced version that will have a relatively short-learning period, facilitating fast analysis of large models and convincing graphic output. It will be made commercially available, allowing a much wider range of designers to become directly involved in tensile-structure design.

14 A parallel can be made with the development of structures built out of cast and wrought iron during the eighteenth and nineteenth centuries which did not lead to the cessation of developments in timber building techniques.

Softness – Architectural Body Language

1 Bodo Rasch, 'Architectural Umbrellas', *Tensile Structures, Architectural Design* (London), 1995, p25. Rasch describes here the importance of interactive design procedures used in creating tensile structures, in particular the folding-umbrella-type system at the Prophet's Holy Mosque, Medina, Saudia Arabia, 1992.

2 To some extent architectural schools can be blamed for this, as in many programmes design integration that relates engineering and building forms hardly exists. Another factor is the problems associated with communicating innovative techniques to the design professions and industry. In the US much of the research is advanced, however, most is privately sponsored by industry which is then protective of its investment. UK research tends to take place in an academic environment more frequently, which encourages the exchange of information. However, academic research possesses inherent difficulties in bringing good work to the application stage.

3 It is believed that the Colosseum in Rome, AD70-82, had a canvas canopy called a *velarium*.

4 Hugo Häring, 'Approaches to Form' (1925), quoted in Kenneth Frampton, *Modern Architecture: A Critical History*, 3rd edition, Thames and Hudson (London), 1992, p122. Frampton describes Häring's buildings as 'naively imitative of biological form'.

5 Dalland stated, 'a building can be considered a "body" and its visual appearance can be considered as "non-verbal, intuitable information"', in 'The Body Language of Tensile Structures', a paper given at the ASCE Structures Congress XII, 1994, in conjunction with the IASS International Symposium, Atlanta, GA.

6 Buro Happold have done the same for the UK tent-rental industry.

7 Most traditional touring circus tents were much smaller than this. At the turn of the century Barnum and Bailey's 'Greatest Show on Earth' was just that – a huge entertainment spectacular that toured Europe with a tent measuring 54 x 130 metres, which seated up to 10,000 people. See Robert Kronenburg, *Houses in Motion: The Genesis, History and Development of the Portable Building*, Academy Editions (London), 1995, p37.

8 Earlier in the twentieth century, the sculptural quality of tensile structures was extensively explored by Naum Gabo; tensile membranes have also been the main medium of installation-artist Maurice Agis. See Robert Kronenburg, *Portable Architecture*, Architectural Press (Oxford), 1996, pp108-15.

9 In 'A Portable Architecture for the Next Millenium', a paper presented at the Fifth International Architectural Forum, held in Prague, in May 1996, Goldsmith stated: 'The evolution of the history of architecture has been a slow process from mass to membrane. We are at the precipice of a moment when this process will accelerate.' (Goldsmith, here was quoting Bill Katavolos 'architecture is moving from mass to membrane'.)

Movement – Event Space

1 Charles Eames from a lecture to the American Academy of Art and Science, quoted by Nicholas Goldsmith in 'Structure and Lightness', *Interior View*, 5 January 1994, pp77-79.

2 The term 'portable' has been used to describe all types of movable buildings since the nineteenth century and this practice is continued here.

3 For a more detailed exploration of the range and pattern of transportable building types see Robert Kronenburg, *Houses in Motion*.

4 Fuller was in this case referring to the Wichita House, the promise of which was never fulfilled. Buckminster Fuller, 'Designing a New Industry' in James Mellor (ed), *The Buckminster Fuller Reader*, Cape (London), 1970, p169.

5 Keith Goddard of exhibition designers Studio Works prepared the material.

Light – Softness and Movement

1 Italo Calvino in *Six Memos for the Next Millennium*, quoted by Nicholas Goldsmith in 'Structure and Lightness', *Interior View*, 5 January 1994, pp77-79. Goldsmith adds that this suggests 'that our desire to pare down to the essential, be it in literature, art, music or architecture, comes from a need to balance the weight and burdens associated with our modern lives'.

2 Sensitively designed steel and concrete structures can also be made to express these forces, however, it is impossible to design membrane structures in any other way.

3 Nicholas Goldsmith has also prepared a new lighting concept for Sunar Hausermann, creating office interiors based solely on light diffused through fabric membranes.

COLLABORATORS & STAFF

Former

Ross Dalland
Denis Hector
Julian Cripps
Tim Culvahouse
Belinda Watts
Charles Mendler
Gisela Stromeyer
Sarah Bonnesmaison
Amedeo Perlas
Inson Wood
Ronn Basquette
Sam Armijos
Ali Tayar
Bill Murrell
Peter Heppel
Robert Dickey
Tina Gieger
Mike Meyer
Rudi Scheurmann
Andrew Formichella
Izumi Shepard
Julian King
Paul Romain
Andrea Janeke-Schroeder
Dana Cook
Harold Holsberg
Paul Westbury
Angus Palmer

Present

David Burke
Andre Chaszar
Judy Choi
Todd Dalland
Stanislas Gaweda
Irvin Glassman
Nicholas Goldsmith
Mercedes Gonzalez
Stephanie Hellmuth
Tom LaGreca
Bill Lenart
Robert Lerner
Sui Ming Louie
Bryan Morrison
Evelyn Natal
Sharon Pell-Lie
Robert Riley
Wayne Rendely
Felicity Reynard
Craig Schwitter
Numer Ybanez

CHRONOLOGY

1976	St Michael's Montessori Playground, NYC
1977	Camp Wayne Pavilion, Preston, PA
1977	Norwalk In-Water Boat Show, Connecticut
1978	Anchor Modules System, Evansville, IN
1978	Goldsmith Loft Tent, NYC
1978	Skylight Vela Residence, NYC
1979	White House Ellipse Canopies, Washington, DC
1979	Aspen Windstar, Aspen, CO
1979	National Symphony Orchestra Acoustical Shell, Washington, DC
1980	Sopers Ltd System 100, Hamilton, Ontario
1980	Dolphin Pool at Canada's Wonderland, Toronto
1980	Kuwait Amphitheater
1980	State University of New York @ Purchase, Acoustical Shell, NY
1980	Rotork Pavilion, Poole, UK
1981	Pier Six Concert Pavilion, Baltimore, MD
1981	Starlight Theater, Kansas City, MD
1981	Claude Montana Tunnel, NYC
1982	Studio 54 Entrance, NYC
1983	Florida National Pavilion, Jacksonville, FL
1983	Brooklyn Aquarium Dolphin Pool, NYC
1983	Biederman Gala, NYC
1984	Pensacola Swimming Pool, FL
1984	Interiors Initiative, *Interiors* magazine
1984	Anchor Bandshell, Evansville, IN
1985	Bradford Exchange Offices and Exhibition, Chicago, IL
1985	Donna Karan Showroom, NYC
1985	Art on the Beach '85, NYC
1985	Procter & Gamble Performance Pavilion at Sawyer Point, Cincinnati, OH
1985	Miami Center for the Arts Retractable, FL
1985	Harvard Commencement Pavilion
1985	Lake Tahoe Performance Pavilion, CA
1985	Sunar Hauserman office installation, NYC
1986	Baltimore Aquarium Queuing Pavilion, MD
1986	Roseland Ballroom Renovation, NYC
1986	Harvard Architecture Review
1986	Cleveland Convention Center Ceiling, OH
1987	World Financial Center Winter Garden Performance Structures, NYC
1987	China Grill Lighting, NYC
1987	'We The People' Pavilion, Philadelphia, PA
1987	Issey Miyake, Windows, Bergdorf Goodman's, NYC
1987	South Street Seaport Bandshell, NYC
1987	Valentino Boutique, Great Neck, NY
1987	Isle of Wight Concert Pavilion, MD
1987	Beige & Co Showroom, NYC
1988	Stortz Hypars, Miami
1988	Greenwich Acoustic Shell, CT
1988	Central Park Summer Stage, NYC
1988	Charles Ives Center Audience Retractable Roof, CT
1988	Omni/Guggenheim Museum Mobiles, NYC
1988	Pickle Family Circus Tent, San Francisco, CA
1988	Isetan Boutique, Singapore
1989	Caramoor Theater, Katonah, NY
1989	World Financial Center Ferry Terminal, NYC
1990	Dolphin Hotel Atrium, Orlando, FL
1990	Anchor New Century System Tents, Evansville, IN
1990	MOTCO Trust Air Structure, Houston, TX
1990	Eureka! Camping Tents
1990	Olympia & York Pylons, NYC
1990	Armbruster Tent System
1990	Greenwich Performance Pavilion, CT
1990	US Army, New Family of General Purpose Tents, Natick, MA
1990	Vitra Shop Exhibit, NYC
1990	World Financial Center Ferry Terminal, NYC
1990-96	DKNY Headquarters, NYC
1991	Carlos Moseley Music Pavilion, NYC
1991	Pier Six Concert Pavilion, Baltimore, MD
1991	Phoenix Central Library sunshades
1992	Carmelo Pomodoro Offices and Showroom, NYC
1992	Jeddah Hotel Competition, Saudi Arabia
1992	Calvin Klein Co Showrooms, NYC
1992	Kiamesha Performing Arts Facility, Kiamesha, NY
1993	Pyramid Entertainment Traveling Arena
1993	Finnish Chancery Walkway Canopy, Washington, DC
1993	Norton McNaughton Headquarters, NYC
1993	Seventh on 6th Fashion Village, Bryant Park, NYC
1993	McAllen Center, TX

1993-95	US Army Air-Inflated Building Systems, Natick, MA
1994	Takashimaya Boutique, NYC
1994	MOMRA Penthouse, Riyadh, Saudi Arabia
1994	Boston Harborlights Pavilion, Boston, MA
1994	The Time for Peace Traveling Pavilion
1994	Trading Floor interior, Metlife Building, NYC
1994	Columbus Circle Retail Pavilion, NYC
1994	UNFPA–UN World Population Fund Exhibit
1994	Eureka! Capri System, Binghamton, NY
1994	Club Smirnoff Traveling Exhibition
1995	National Video Editing Facility, Wesport, CT
1995	Cadillac Exceleration Center
1995	New Phoenix Library sunshades, AZ
1995	Finnish Chancery Walkway Canopy, Washington, DC
1995	Ringling Consultancy – Traveling Arena for Ringling Bros Barnum & Bailey
1995	Indianapolis Arts Garden Performance Pavilion
1995	Beirut Exhibition Pavilion, Beirut, Lebanon
1996	SHIK Health & Sport Club, Kuwait
1996	Staten Island Esplanade, NYC
1996	San Diego Aerospace Museum, CA
1996	'Look of the Games', 1996 Olympics, Atlanta, GA
1996	AT&T Global Olympic Village, Atlanta, GA
1996	Atlanta Olympic Games, Atlanta, GA
1996	Bigio Residence, NYC
1996	Spectrum Glazing
1996	Darien Lake Amphitheater, Buffalo, NY
1997	Cirque De Soleil at Disney World, Orlando, FL
1997	Dejur Aviary, Bronx Zoo, NYC
1997	Korean Assembly, NYC
1997	Truck-mounted Retractable Bandshell
1997	Andrea Jovine Headquarters, NYC
1997	Cancun Roof Structure, Cancun, Mexico
1997	Westin Hotel Retractable Roof, Washington, DC
1997	Grand Central Station Tensile Structures, NYC
1997	Remsberg Tent System, Frederick, MD
1997	Sofri Mall, Iquique, Chile
1997	Duta Plaza, Kuala Lumpur
1998	Castle Clinton Renovation, NYC
1998	Under the Sun, Photovoltaic Show at National Design Museum, NYC

AWARDS

1980 Since 1980, FTL Associates has been the recipient of over forty International Design Awards sponsored by Industrial Fabrics Association International (IFAI).

1985 International Association of Lighting Designers Award (IALD) for the Donna Karan Showroom.

1986 State of Florida's Governor's Design Award for the Florida National Pavilion, Jacksonville, FL.

1987 Lumen Award for the Tensil Lighting System, an integrated lighting system product.

1989 Interiors Award (*Interiors* magazine) in Recreation & Entertainment for the World Financial Center Winter Garden Performance Space.

1989 New York State Council on the Arts (NYSCA) Grant Award for Surface Forms Research Group.

1990 Waterfront Center's Award for the Bicentennial Commons at Sawyer Point Park, Cincinnati, Ohio.

1992 14th Annual Interiors Award (*Interiors* magazine) for 'Best in Showroom Design' for the Carmelo Pomodoro Showroom and Offices.

1992 ID 'Environments' Award. For the DKNY Showroom building.

1992 Winner of the Kuwait Health Club Invited Competition for a two-million-square-foot health club facility.

1992 Metal Construction Association Honor Award for the DKNY Headquarters.

1992 New York State AIA Award for Excellence in Design for the DKNY Headquarters.

1992 Record Interiors Award (*Architectural Record* magazine) for 'Excellence in Planning and Design'.

1993 'Emerging Voice' from the NY Architectural League.

1994 Boston Harborlights Pavilion 'Best New Major Concert Venue' by *Pollstar Magazine* at the 1994 Concert Industry Awards.

1995 28th Bard Award for Excellence in Architecture and Urban Design for the Carlos Moseley Music Pavilion.

1996 USITT (United States Institute for Theater Technology) Award of Merit for the Carlos Moseley Music Pavilion.

1996 Todd Dalland's contribution to architecture was acknowledged with a Fellowship in the American Institute of Architects (FAIA).

1996 Third prize in the design competition for the platform roofing of Helsinki Railway Station.

1997 Nicholas Goldsmith's contribution to architecture was acknowledged with a Fellowship in the American Institute of Architects (FAIA).

EXHIBITIONS

1983 'Architecture Group Show' curated by Andrew McNair at PS 1, New York.

1984 'Furnishings by Architects', Max Protech Gallery, New York.

1985 Art on the Beach, 'Sign/Stage: A Podium for Dissent', collaboration with the artist Dennis Adams and performing artist Ann Magnuson for Creative Time Inc, New York.

1985 'Making Shelter – Exhibition and Symposium', Harvard Graduate School of Design, Department of Architecture, Cambridge, MA.

1990 Mondo Materialis at the Pacific Design Center and the Cooper-Hewitt Museum, New York.

1990 'The Pup Tent', Doghouse Exhibition at the Cooper-Hewitt Museum, New York.

1992 'A New American Flag', Max Protech Gallery, New York.

1993 'Architecture & Lightness' a travelling exhibition displayed at the Vialle delle Scienze in Palermo and at the Naples Royal Palace, Italy.

1997 'Portable Architecture', RIBA Architecture Centre, London

1997 'Spontaneous Construction', The Building Centre, London.

1998 'Under the Sun', FTL is the designer for this exhibition showcasing photo-voltaic technology in design and architecture, Cooper Hewitt National Design Museum, summer.

BIBLIOGRAPHY

FTL PUBLICATIONS AND ARTICLES

Armijos, Samuel J, 'Going Mobile', *Fabrics & Architecture* (St Paul, Minnesota), vol 3, 1991:1 (May/June), pp16-19.

Armijos, Samuel J, 'Textile Architecture Education', *Fabrics & Architecture* (St Paul, Minnesota), vol 6, 1994:4 (July/August).

Arnaboldi, Mario Antonio, 'A Tent in Baltimore', *l'ARCA* (Milan, Italy), 1995:98 (November), pp72-75.

Barreneche, Raul A, 'Building in Glass', *Architecture* (New York), (1996:12), pp114-15.

Bartolini, Clara, 'Uffici d'Autore: Donna Karan, New York', *OFX Office International #20*, Design Diffusion Edizioni srl (Milan, Italy), September/October 1994. (Italian publication).

Boles, Daralice Donkervoet, 'Rites of Passage', *Metropolis* (New York), January/February 1984.

Burczyk, Mary, 'FTL – A Successful Blend of Architecture, Engineering and Hard Work', *Industrial Fabrics Products Review* (St Paul, Minnesota), 1983:10.

Christ, Ronald and Dennis Dollens, *New York Nomadic Design*, ed Gustavo Gili SA, Rizzoli International Publications (New York), 1993, pp16 & 34-35.

Cook, Jean M, 'The Fabstruct Challenge', *Fabrics & Architecture* (St Paul, Minnesota), vol 6, 1994:4 (July/August).

'Creative Tension: FTL Associates', US Design Profiles, *Interior Design* (New York), 1989:9.

Currimbhoy, Nayana, 'Light Games at the Olympics', *Architectural Record* Lighting, supplement to *Architectural Record* (New York), (1996:11), pp18-20.

Curtis, William JR 'Desert Illumination, Phoenix Central Library', *Architecture* (New York), vol 84, 1995:10, pp56-65.

Dalland, Todd, 'The Design Process', International Symposium on Architectural Fabric Structures, vol 1,1984:11.

Dalland, Todd, 'Developing Standards in the Rental Tent Industry', *Industrial Fabrics Products Review* (St Paul, Minnesota), 1987:3.

Dalland, Todd, 'Structural Detailing', *l'ARCA* (Milan, Italy), 1993:73 (July/August). (Italian publication).

Dalland, Todd, 'A Foster Future Bodes Well For Fabrics', *Fabrics & Architecture* (St Paul, Minnesota), vol 6, 1994:3 (May/June).

Dalland, Todd, 'The Body Language of Tensile Structures', proceedings of the ASCE Structures Congress XII in conjunction with the IASS International Symposium, Atlanta, GA, 1994.

Dunlap, David W, 'Philharmonic and Met. Await an Unusual Stage', *New York Times*, 24 June 1989.

'Fabric Gives Baltimore Harbor New Life', *Industrial Fabric Products Review* (St Paul, Minnesota), (1982:3).

Fabric Membrane Tension Structures in Architecture, Maggioli Editore, 1993, pp15, 24, 30, 140, 165-67, 188-89 and 191. (Italian publication).

'Fabric Structure To Be Explored', *Design News*, 19 November 1984.

'Fabric Weaves its Way into AIA Expo 96', news section, *Fabrics & Architecture* (St Paul, Minnesota), vol 8, 1996:4 (July), p6.

Filler, Martin, 'Tents for Interiors, Ellipses, and Music', *Progressive Architecture* (Cleveland, Ohio), 1979:9.

Fisher, Thomas, 'Computers: The Professional Adjusts, FTL/SOM', *Progressive Architecture* (Cleveland, Ohio), 1985:5.

Fisher, Thomas, 'Up on the Roof', *Progressive Architecture* (Cleveland, Ohio), vol 12 (1992:12), pp54-57.

Friedman, Arthur (with contributions from Constance CR White and Janet Ozzard), *Women's Wear Daily* (New York), 'CFDA to Pitch All Its Tents in Bryant Park in November', vol 166, 1993:23 (3 August).

'FTL Architects Featured in Interiors Magazine', *Cornell Architecture Art & Planning Newsletter* (New York), fall 1995.

Gardner, James B, 'Fabric Structure Pioneers Look Back – and Envision the Future', *Architectural Record* (New York), 1985:3.

Gardner, Liese, 'A Sculpted Event', *Special Events* (Culver City, California), 1988:6.

Gardner, Liese, 'American Galas: Scene About Town', *Special Events* (Culver City, California), 1989:1.

Gault, Ylonda, 'Architects with big eye on Waterfront', *Craines New York Business* (New York), vol III, 1992:50 (14-20 December), p34.

Gillitt, William, 'Current Design Development: Baltimore's Outdoor Concert Pavilion', *Federal Design Matters*, winter 1981.

Goldsmith, Nicholas, 'The Design Process', *International Symposium on Architectural Fabric Structures*, vol 1, 1984:11.

Goldsmith, Nicholas, 'The Shell Game: Performing Alfresco on any Budget', *Symphony Magazine* (Washington, DC), October/November 1986.

Goldsmith, Nicholas, 'Tensile Structures Present Unique Lighting Design Options, Opportunities, Potentials', *Architectural Lighting* (Eugene, Oregon), 1988:11.

Goldsmith, Nicholas, 'Tensile Structures', *Housing: Symbol, Structure, Site*, ed Lisa Taylor, Cooper Hewett Museum, Rizzoli (New York), 1990, pp136-37.

Goldsmith, Nicholas, 'The Peripatetic Pavilion', *Design Quarterly* (Minneapolis, Minnesota), summer 1992, pp28-32.

Goldsmith, Nicholas, 'Architecture and Lightness', *Interior View*, United Publishers SA (Paris), 1994:5 (January). (French publication in English).

Gould, Kira, 'An American in Beirut', *Metropolis* (New York), vol 15, 1995:4 (November), p22.

Graham, Beryl, 'Long-term Relationships/Photography as Permanent Public Art', *Camerawork*, vol 20, 1993:2 (fall/winter).

Gunts, Edward, 'Pier 6 Reappears on Music Scene: New concert pavilion boasts more space, better facilities', *The Sun: Arts & Entertainment* (Baltimore, Maryland), 21 July 1991.

Harriman, Marc S, 'Strike Up the Bandstand', *Architecture* (New York), (1991:9), pp102-05.

Hatton, EM, *The Tent Book*, The Houghton Mifflin Company (Boston, Massachusetts), 1979, pp131 and 134.

Henderson, Justin, 'Volumes of Light: The Tensile Lighting System', *Interiors* (New York), 1986:3.

Henderson, Justin, 'New Corporate Style: Stretching the Limits', *Interiors* (New York), 1986:11.

Henderson, Justin, 'Lighting', *Interiors* (New York), 1987:11.

Henderson, Justin, 'Stretched to the Max', *Interiors* (New York), 1989:5.

Henderson, Justin, 'Dramatic Tension', *Interiors* (New York), 1990:1.

Henderson, Justin, 'Sinuous Scenarios', *Interiors* (New York), 1990:7.

'International Association of Lighting Designers 1985 Awards Program', *Architectural Record* (New York), May 1986.

'It's a Cityful of Music, Wall Street to the Park', *New York Times*, 26 August 1990.

Kozinn, Allan, 'A Long Awaited Pavilion Makes Its Debut Tonight', *New York Times*, 20 August 1990.

Kronenburg, Robert, 'Tensile Architecture', *Tensile Structures*, *Architectural Design* (London), 1995: 117, pp8-15.

Kronenburg, Robert, 'Contemporary Design', *Houses in Motion: The Genesis, History and Development of the Portable Building*, Academy Editions (London), 1995, p91.

Kronenburg, Robert, *Portable Architecture*, Architectural Press (Oxford), 1996, pp78-95.

Kurtz, Josh, 'New York's Ambulatory Stage', business section, *The New York Times*, Sunday 16 June 1991.

'Lifestyles: Time for Peace', *Passions International*, vol XVIII, 1994/1995, p16.

Lindgren, Hugo, 'Future Perfect Tents', *Metropolis* (New York), 1991:11, pp28-29.

Louie, Elaine, 'Donna Karan's Penthouse Showroom', *New York Times*, 13 February 1992, section C, p3.

'Making Music in Tents', *Symphony News* (Washinton, DC), 1981:12.

Meisel, Abigail, 'Hoboken Ferry Allows Commuters to Shed "Those Little Town Blues"', *New York Observer*, 29 January 1990.

McKee, Bradford, 'Technology & Practice Info: Tents Showcase New York Fashion Shows', *Architecture* (New York), vol 83, 1994:1.

Melnick, Scott, 'Fabric Structures Find New Markets', *Building Design and Construction*, 1986:5.

Moiraghi, Luigi, 'Un monumento tecnologico – The Phoenix Central Library', *l'ARCA* (Milan, Italy), 1996:103 (April), pp50-57.

Morgan, Jim, 'Tenting the Great Indoors', *Residential Interiors*, March/April 1980.

Morgan, William, 'Diplomatic Community', *The Architectural Review* (London), vol CXCVI, 1994: 1172 (October), pp36-42.

Nesmith, Lynn, 'Harbour Encore', *Architecture* (New York), 1992:9, pp52-55.

'New American Designers', *Abitare* (Milan, Italy), 1986:9.

'News Notes', *Oculus* (Washington, DC), vol 54, 1992:10 (June).

New York Architecture, American Institute of Architects New York Chapter (New York), vol 6, 1993.

'New York, Struttura di protezione solare', *l'ARCA Plus* (Milan, Italy), 1996:8 (May), pp134-37.

'1995 Architectural Showcase: Eastleigh Tennis Centre, the Hampshire Tennis & Health Club', *Athletic Business* (Madison, Wisconsin), vol 19, 1995:6, p110.

'Olympic Moments', showcase section, *Tents Magazine*, vol 3, 1996:3 (fall), pp12-15.

'Panorama', *America Illustrated*,1987:6.

Pearson, Clifford A, 'Fashion Plate', *Architectural Record: Record Interiors* (New York), 1992:9.

Philips, Deborah, 'Bright Lights Big City', *Artnews* (New York), 1985:9.

Pierson, John, 'Form + Function: Tents and Canopies Get Down to Business', *The Wall Street Journal* (New York), 6 September 1990.

Pierson, John, 'Form + Function: Portable Pavilion Opens with Pavorotti Program', *The Wall Street Journal* (New York), 11 June 1991.

Plotkin, Fred, 'Loud and Clear', *Opera News* (New York), June 1991.

'Prototype Demonstrates Possibilities for Modular Work Stations', *Architectural Lighting* (Eugene, Oregon), 1987:6.

Rae, Christine, 'Designers Saturday Tent Show Goes on the Road!', *Leading Edge*, 1986:6.

Rebeck, Gene, 'Tension Structures', *Industrial Fabrics Products Review* (St Paul, Minnesota), 1987:6.

Rebeck, Gene, 'Performance Art', *Fabrics & Architecture* (St Paul, Minnesota), vol 1, 1989:1 (summer).

Rebeck, Gene, 'Future Tense', *Fabrics & Architecture* (St Paul, Minnesota), vol 2, 1990:7.

Rebeck, Gene, 'A Tensile Structure Primer', *Fabrics & Architecture* (St Paul, Minnesota), vol 3, 1991:1 (January/February).

Robbin, Tony, *Engineering a New Architecture*, Yale University Press (New Haven, Connecticut), 1996, pp9, 52 and 54, fig 35.

Russell, Beverly, 'FTL Architects, A Portfolio of Projects', *Interiors* (New York), vol CLV, 1995:3, pp37-66.

Russell, Beverly, 'Getting the Message Out', *Interiors & Sources*, 1996:9.

Scharge, Thomas, 'Fabric Structures Outplace Applications', *Building Design and Construction*, 1988:5.

Sedlak, Vinzenz, 'Membrane Structures: The Design Process', *RIBA Journal* (London), 1985:3.

'Showroom in New York', *Baumeister*, 1993:5, pp30-31. (German publication).

Slesin, Suzanne, 'Experimenting with Indoor Fabric Tents', *New York Times*, 28 May 1981.

Souba, Jane T, 'Works of Art', *Industrial Fabric Products Review* (St Paul, Minnesota), 1989:11.

Takahashi, Masaaki, 'Penthouse Showroom DKNY', 'Display Steelcase Design Partnership', *Wind*, 1993:22 (spring), pp38-41. (Japanese publication).

Taylor, Paul, 'Art On The Beach', *The Face*,1985:9.

Terpening, Susan, 'Breaking New Ground', *Special Events Magazine* (Culver City, California), vol 15, 1996:7 (July), pp26-27 and 30-31.

'The 16th Annual Interiors Awards', *Interiors* (New York), vol CLIV, 1995:1, pp84-88.

Toy, Maggie, 'Four Projects by FTL', Tensile Structures, *Architectural Design* (London), 1995: 117, pp42-48.

'Uber den Dachern von Manhattan', *Textil-Wirtschaft*, 1992:9 (27 February). (German publication).

Vandenberg, Maritz, *Soft Canopies – Detail in Building*, Academy Editions (London), 1996, pp13, 22 and 54-61.

Vickers, Graham, 'Face to Face: Future Tents', *World Architecture* (London), 1995:35 (April), pp106-09.

Vilades, Pilar, 'Stretching the Limits', *Progressive Architecture* (Cleveland, Ohio), 1987:9.

Vogel, Carol, 'The Test of Time: Are Today's Architecturally Inspired Pieces Tomorrow's Classics?', *New York Times Magazine*, 1984:12.

Wagner, Michael, 'Fabric Architecture: FTL Architects fashion a showroom for Carmelo Pomodoro', *Interiors* (New York), 1993:1.

Weathersby, Jr, William, 'In Tents Fashion', *Lighting Dimensions*, vol 18, 1994:3 (April).

White, Constance CR, 'DKNY: A Home of Its Own', *Women's Wear Daily* (New York), 12 February 1992, p12

Wilson, Forrest, 'Penthouse Showroom: Fashion Factory, New York City', *Blueprints: The Magazine of the National Building Museum*, vol XI, 1993:2 (spring), p7.

Woodruff, Mark, 'Architecture Under Wraps: Rethinking the Tent', *Taxi* (1989:4).

TV and Video

Architects of Style, 'Videofashion Monthly', vol 20, 9 November 1995. 24 minutes.

'AT&T Global Olympic Village', VNR, B-Roll and Soundbites, 18 July 1996.

'AT&T Global Olympic Village', VNR Package, Rough Edit, 15 July 1996.

'Bloomberg SmallBusiness', Bloomberg Television and Radio, USA Network, 6.00 am, 12 October 1996.

'NBC Weekend Today' (AT&T Global Olympic Village VNR, live interview), 21 July 1996.

7th Avenue Shows, 'Videofashion News', vol 20, 11 November 1995. 4 minutes.

Temporary Buildings, 'News Science & Technology', CNN TV, 11.00 am, 29 June 1996. 5.43 minutes.

General Bibliography

Banham, Reyner, *Theory and Design in the First Machine Age*, Architectural Press (London), 1960.

Banham, Reyner, *The Architecture of the Well-Tempered Environment*, 2nd edition, (Chicago), 1984.

Addis, Bill, *Tension Structures* exhibition catalogue, Building Centre Trust (London), 1976.

Drew, Philip, *Frei Otto: Form and Structure*, Crosby Lockwood Stopes (London), 1976.

Frampton, Kenneth, *Modern Architecture: A Critical History*, 3rd edition, Thames and Hudson (London), 1992.

Fuller, Buckminster, Mellor, James (ed), *The Buckminster Fuller Reader*, (London), 1970.

Goldsmith, Nicholas, 'Structure and Lightness', *Interior View*, 5 January 1996.

Goldsmith, Nicholas, 'A Portable Architecture for the Next Millenium', Fifth International Architectural Forum, Prague, May 1996.

Happold, Ted, 'Chariots of Fire', *Tensile Structures*, *Architectural Design* (London), 1995: 117.

Happold, Thomas and Eve Mathew, *In Memorium*.

Kronenburg, Robert, 'Tensile Architecture', *Tensile Structures*, *Architectural Design* (London), 1995: 117.

Kronenburg, Robert, *Houses in Motion: The Genesis, History and Development of the Portable Building*, Academy Editions (London), 1995.

Kronenburg, Robert, *Portable Architecture*, Architectural Press (Oxford), 1996.

Oliver, Paul, *Shelter Sign and Symbol*, Barrie and Jenkins (London), 1975.

Pawley, Martin, *Theory and Design in the Second Machine Age*, Basil Blackwell (Oxford), 1990.

Rapoport, Amos, *House Form and Culture*, Prentice Hall (New Jersey), 1969.

Roland, Conrad, *Frei Otto: Tension Structures*, originally published by Verlag Ullstein (Berlin, West Germany), translated by CV Amerongen for Longman Group (London), Praeger Publications Inc (New York and Washington), 1970.

Rudofsky, Bernard, *Architecture without Architects*, Museum of Modern Art (New York), 1965.

Shelter, *Shelter Publications* (Bolinas, California), 1973.